Lessons and Lovers

D. H. Lawrence in New Mexico

A play

Olwen Wymark

Samuel French - London

New York — Sydney - Toronto - Hollywood

ISBN 0 573 01644 5

LESSONS AND LOVERS

Commissioned by and first performed at York Theatre
Royal in November, 1985.

Frieda Lawrence	Jennie Stoller
Mabel Dodge Luhan	Patricia England
The Hon. Dorothy Brett	Amanda Grinling
D. H. Lawrence	Benny Young
Professor	Adrian Lukis
Students	Lisa David
	Anna Gilbert
	Lawrence Evans
	Dean Hollingsworth

Directed by Andrew McKinnon
Designed by Vikie le Sache
Lighting designed by Tim Thornalley

CHARACTERS

D. H. Lawrence	Tall and thin, red hair and beard. Speaks with slight North Country accent. Arrogant, tempestuous and often violently bad tempered but also affectionatee, kind and witty
Frieda Lawrence	Born the Baronness von Richthofen. A fat, genial, handsome lioness of a woman who can be as domineering and hot tempered as Lawrence but is generally warm and easygoing. Marked Austrian accent
The Honourable Dorothy Brett	Young-looking and quite pretty though chinless and pop-eyed. Posh accent and background (dancing lessons with Queen Victoria's grandchildren as a child) but also a hard worker on the ranch. Hunts and fishes rather well; paints rather badly
Mabel Dodge Luhan	A literary American headhunter married (her fourth marriage) to a Pueblo Indian. Affected and pretentious but is also warmhearted and generous; and rich. Not tall but quite plump and attractive
The Professor	Typical East-coast academic anywhere between thirty and fifty
The Students	Post-graduates from University of New Mexico. Two women, two men

The women are all in their early forties for most of the play but also in their fifties and sixties for some of the scenes

The play is set in New Mexico on the Lawrences' ranch, Kiowa (pronounced to rhyme with Iowa) and the action takes place between the years 1922 and 1945 and also in the present day

Lawrence is in his late thirties and, at the end of the play, forty-four

My thanks to Keith Sagar for his help concerning copyright material and whose books on Lawrence were of great value to me in researching and writing the play.

Thanks, too, to Gerald Pollinger Ltd. and the Estate of Mrs Frieda Lawrence Ravagli for permission to include the copyright material.

My most particular thanks to Andrew McKinnon without whose encouragement and support this play would probably never have been written.

O. W.

ACT I*

In the darkness the sound of the comfortable laughter of three women

Frieda Oh Mabel, you're making it up.

Mabel I'm not I swear to God. He said——

Brett Do keep still, Mabel.

Mabel Sorry, Brett. No but really, Frieda, this man said he knew for a fact that just before Lorenzo died he was made supreme chief of the Pueblo Indians. He wanted to buy a photograph of him in his tribal robes.

Frieda (*laughing*) You can see him. All in feathers.

Brett He would have looked beautiful.

Mabel Oh he would not, Brett. Much too skinny. And that red beard!

The Lights have been coming up very slowly. Frieda and Mabel are sitting on the steps of the Lawrences' wooden house on their ranch in New Mexico. Brett sits a little distance away, sketching them. She wears an old-fashioned hearing aid. Frieda is smoking and Mabel is posing for Brett. It's nineteen forty-five and they're all in their sixties. A wide beautiful sky is behind them and the house is represented in a skeletal way so that we can see the sky behind. Near the house is the corral fence and there is a rather crudely made wooden chair with painted decorations standing downstage

Also revealed by the gradually increasing light are three figures in silhouette who are quite still. These are Students I, II and III

Frieda So what did your Tony say about how it turns out Lorenzo was the supreme chief of his tribe?

Mabel I didn't dare tell him.

Lawrence (*shouting, off, in the distance*) Frieda!

No-one on stage reacts to this

Brett All these damnfool people coming up here with their damnfool questions. Mabel, you moved again.

Mabel Oh dear. Like this?

Frieda Ja ja, Brett is right. They should just stay at home and read his

---

* N.B. Paragraph 3 on page ii of this Acting Edition regarding photocopying and video-recording should be carefully read.

books. Stupid tourists. What they like is all the lies and scandals they've
heard about Lorenzo and me. They don't care about his genius.

Mabel Well it's your own fault the tourists come, Frieda. They all want to
see that hideous chapel you built.

Frieda Oh bosh, Mabel. Anyway it's not a chapel, it's a shrine, with
Lorenzo's phoenix carved on the top and the beautiful decorations Brett
did inside. He would have loved it.

Lawrence (*shouting, off*) Brett!

Again there is no reaction

Frieda And how could I have left him buried in Europe? Ach, this terrible
war.

Mabel Oh Frieda, the war's been over for weeks now.

Frieda It's different for you. You're not German.

Brett Well neither are you. You were British for years and now you're
American. What I'm worried about is whether that dreadful little Labour
Government's going to let me take my money out of England.

Mabel The thing is, Lorenzo's books are hard to get hold of nowadays.
That's why people don't read them.

Brett Oh codswallop. They could get them if they wanted to. Libraries and
places.

Mabel I'm only saying they aren't being published any more. A lot of the
younger people haven't even heard of him.

Frieda And they are exactly the ones who should read him! They would
understand what he wanted this ranch to be. Everyone living and working
together and writing books and poems and painting and making sculp-
tures.

Brett (*smiling over at Frieda*) Rananim.

Lawrence (*shouting, off*) Mabel!

Again no reaction

Frieda Ja, Rananim. Poor Lorenzo, he always had that dream. Never came
true.

*At some point during the last few speeches, Student I has walked over to the
steps and gone up them between Mabel and Frieda who are totally unaware of
him. He has been standing and gazing round in the house and now he comes
down the steps again*

Student I The house is still the same as when the Lawrences lived in it. Even
the furniture. (*He goes over to the wooden chair*) He made this chair
himself.

Brett Oh it did come true, Frieda. When we first came here.

Mabel No, Frieda's right. It wasn't what he meant.

Frieda Like when we tried in Cornwall, Lawrence and me. With Katherine
and Murry. Too much squabbling.

Brett Well, but do you remember how we used to sit around and sing in the
evenings in the old days here?

Frieda Ach yes, Lorenzo always sang.

Frieda hums and then sings a German folksong. Mabel and Brett join in

Mabel (*breaking off*) Brett! You're out of tune.

Frieda (*laughing*) She always was.

Brett Not always.

Frieda (*affectionately*) Always.

Student II There's a fellowship the University gives for somebody to come up here and live in this house for six months and write a paper.

Frieda He knew this second war would come, you know. He said so on Armistice Day in nineteen eighteen. On that very day. Nobody listened. We were at a party in Gordon Square.

Mabel Speaking of parties, I'm sorry, Brett, but I'll have to go. I've still got loads of things to do for tonight. Is Angelino going to be back in time, Frieda?

Frieda Oh ja ja, I'm sure. You know him, he never wants to miss a party. Especially your big Thanksgiving dinner.

Mabel The first Thanksgiving since the war! Tony's asked some of the other Indians to come up after dinner. They're going to dance the peace dances.

Frieda Oh good. Lovely.

Brett Don't move yet, Mabel. Just a minute more. (*As she works*) Anyway you don't have to do anything. Your servants do all the work.

Student III Be lonely living up here all by yourself.

Student II How could you be lonely? There's conferences and seminars and faculty weekends and stuff going on practically the whole year round.

Mabel (*annoyed*) They have to be told what to do, you know. Organized. I'm the one that has to make all the decisions. Not that you know the first thing about being a hostess. (*She gets up*) Oh honestly, I get stiffer every week.

Frieda So do I. (*She laughs*) We're so old.

Brett I don't feel any older at all.

Mabel You! You've always refused to grow up.

Frieda The eternal débutante.

Brett Don't. I detested all that. Ugh. Those ghastly dances.

Frieda Oh I loved dancing.

Student I (*pointing out toward the audience*) That's that pine tree where he used to sit and write.

Mabel (*looking at Brett's picture*) Nice, Brett. You've made Frieda awfully thin, though.

Frieda Oh good let's see. Oh. Why do I have to be smoking?

Brett You always are. I'm putting Lorenzo here. Sitting against the pine tree, writing.

Mabel But the tree isn't behind the house. It's down there.

Brett Artistic licence.

Student III Look, you can see the desert from up here. And the Rockies.

Frieda (*ruefully*) He'd be sixty.

Mabel (*sadly*) Can you imagine.

Brett (*romantic*) Silver hair, silver beard.

Frieda and Mabel exchange an amused look

Frieda You know sometimes I think what I should do is leave this ranch to the New Mexico University in my will.
Brett Why on earth?
Frieda Oh well ... they could study up here. Young people coming and working on the ranch and writing and painting ... reading Lorenzo's books.
Brett (*laughing*) Oh I see. They could be Rananim.
Frieda (*laughing too*) Ja.
Mabel But you wouldn't really, would you, Frieda?
Frieda I might.
Mabel Angelino wouldn't let you.
Frieda Let? Let? It's my ranch!
Mabel All right, all right. Brett, do you want to drive down to Taos with me now?
Brett No, I'm going to do some work. Did I tell you that woman definitely wants one of the big pictures?
Frieda No! *Wunderbar!*
Mabel You be sure she pays you a good price.
Frieda (*kissing them*) *Wiedersehen*, Brett. Mabel.
Brett Toodle pip. (*Then as she starts to go*) Oh Frieda, do you think Angie would come and have a look at the skylight in the studio? It's sticking again.
Frieda Sure. I'll tell him.
Mabel Bye Brett. See you later, Frieda.

Mabel and Brett exit in different directions

Frieda goes out through the house

The Students are still looking out

After a moment or so, the Professor enters

Professor Oh, you're here. I'm rounding people up for the reading.
Student III What time does it start?
Professor In about ten minutes. It's in the main seminar room. I'm just going to check and see if people are still in the cafeteria.

The Professor goes off in one direction, the Students go off in the other

The Lights fade to a Black-out

Lawrence enters during the Black-out

Lawrence (*in the darkness*) Brett!

The Lights come up on Lawrence, centre stage. After a moment, he calls again

Brett? Where've you got to?

Brett runs on, breathless

Brett I'm here, Lorenzo. I was just going to fetch the wood.

Lawrence (*indignantly*) What did you say?
Brett (*getting out the ear trumpet*) What did you say?
Lawrence Just going? You mean you've not got it yet?
Brett But Lorenzo, I was catching the cow. You——
Lawrence Did you get her?
Brett (*pleased with herself*) Yes I did.
Lawrence I should think so too. (*Irritably*) Well get on then, Brett, get on. That oven's got to be kept red hot you know and I'm almost out of wood. Off with you.
Brett I'll be as quick as I can.

Brett dashes off

Lawrence (*calling after her*) Bring a lot!

Mabel enters, dragging a large branch of a tree with leaves on it

Mabel I've got some wood, Lorenzo.
Lawrence That's no good, Mabel, it's green. Can't you see? It'll only smoke.
Mabel (*disappointed; dropping the branch*) Oh.
Lawrence Don't just leave it there. Bring it over to the yard.

Lawrence gives Mabel a hand and they start dragging the branch off

All these years living on a ranch and you still don't know green wood doesn't burn. You're too rich and spoiled, Mabel, that's your trouble. Look at Brett. She's never lived this kind of life before but she——
Mabel (*angry*) Oh Brett's perfect, of course!
Lawrence Mabel . . . you promised you weren't——
Mabel (*hastily humble*) Sorry, Lorenzo.
Lawrence I can't understand why you three women are always at each other. Squabble squabble squabble. It's easy enough to be peaceful and——

Frieda enters, brandishing a dead chicken

Frieda (*aggressively*) What's this?
Mabel Really, Frieda. It's a chicken.
Frieda Mind your own business, Mabel.
Mabel Oh, delightful!
Lawrence It's our supper.
Frieda (*angry*) My hen. My Smoky.
Lawrence You'd better hurry up and pluck her. She can go into the oven after I've finished baking the bread.
Frieda How could you kill her?
Lawrence How? How? I wrung her neck, that's how. She was getting broody. I hate them when they're like that. Anyway it'll be nice to have chicken for once instead of——
Frieda Oh yes, oh yes. Kill her because she wants some babies. Of course, slaughter her. Not allowed! We mustn't have——
Lawrence Shut up, Frieda.
Frieda Why should I?

Lawrence Because I say so! *Basta!* Come on, Mabel.

Frieda tries to speak again but Lawrence drowns her out, clucking loudly like a chicken

    Lawrence and Mabel exit, Mabel giggling

    Brett enters, with a big armload of firewood

Brett (*hurrying across the stage*) Has the fire in the oven gone out?
Frieda I don't know. How should I know? Here. (*She puts the chicken on top of Brett's load*) Tell him he can pluck his own damn supper. I'm going for a walk.

    Frieda goes

Brett (*getting out the ear trumpet*) What? Going where? Frieda, wait ... don't you think you should——?
Lawrence (*off*) Brett! What's happened to the woman?
Brett I'm coming. I'm coming, Lorenzo.

    Brett goes

    The Lights fade to Black-out. Music

    During the Black-out, the Professor and Students enter to one part of the stage, Lawrence and Brett to another

Student IV (*in the darkness*) "Next day was the last. At dawn they put on her a blue robe and led her out into the plaza among the throng of silent dark-blanketed people. There was pure white snow on the ground and the dark people in their dark brown blankets looked like the inhabitants of another world. A large drum was slowly pounding and an old priest was declaiming from a housetop."

The Lights have come up on him. He is reading from a book. The Professor and the other three students are sitting on chairs round him, listening

    "At noon a litter came. She was placed on it and the procession began, led by four feathered dancing priests. Out of the plaza they went, on the trail to the great cottonwood trees that stood like grey silver lace against the blue sky, bare and exquisite above the snow. The strange procession trailed on and on in perpetual dance slowly across the plain towards the mountains. At last she could tell that the dancers were moving forward no more. Above her was a cave like a dark socket halfway up the cliff face. On the platform of the cave the priests waited. They lifted her up and took off her blue robe."

The Lights come up during the next sentence on another part of the stage. Lawrence, sitting on a little stool, holds a notebook on his lap. Brett sits at his feet listening to him

Lawrence ⎱ (*together*) ⎰ "The throng, watching below, gave a low wild cry."
Student IV ⎰   ⎱

Lawrence "Then they laid her on the flat stone, the four powerful men holding her by her outstretched arms and legs. Behind, stood the old priest holding a knife upraised. She felt little sensation though she knew all that was happening. Turning her face to the sky she looked at the yellow sun. It was sinking. She understood now that this was what the men were waiting for, their black eyes watching the sun with glittering eagerness and awe and craving. Their ferocity was ready to leap out into a mystic exultance of triumph when the sun sank. Then the old priest would strike and strike home. Accomplish the sacrifice and achieve the power . . . the mastery that man must hold and that passes from race to race!" *(He closes the notebook)*

Brett *(respectfully, after a pause)* Sorry, Lorenzo, the what? The what that man must hold?

Lawrence *(testily)* The mastery! The mastery! Really, Brett, you said you could hear every word. I asked you and you said you could.

Brett *(hastily)* I could, I could. Only that one. It's a magnificent story, Lorenzo. What will you call it?

Lawrence *The Woman Who Rode Away.*

Frieda *(shouting, off)* Lorenzo!

Frieda enters

Lorenzo, where are you? Ah ha! Of course! I might have known. The curate and the worshipping spinster. Oh how she adores you, eh? And how you adore her adoring you, don't you?

Lawrence All right, Frieda . . . *(He gets up)* I was just reading my new story to Brett.

Frieda And why to Brett? Why not to me?

Lawrence Because you've already read it, you silly gabbler!

Brett gets up and stands gazing off, bored, her ear trumpet down at her side

Frieda So? What difference does that make? Who does she think she is— your muse? Oh lovely . . . ja! You the wonderful noble genius and she is the little handmaiden. She doesn't have to live with you! You and your moods and your horrible nasty tempers.

Lawrence *(going as if to hit her)* Oh be quiet!

Frieda *(dodging; defiantly)* She doesn't have to feed you or wash your clothes or be crazy with fear of your terrible coughing when you spit up blood!

Lawrence flinches. Frieda is shocked at herself

Oh Lorenzo, I didn't——

Brett *(tuning back in; casually)* I'm going back down to my place now, Lorenzo.

Frieda *(with relief, shouting into her ear trumpet)* Good! Go!

Brett turns to go and again takes the ear trumpet from her ear. Frieda pursues her and puts it up to her ear again to shout into it

And stay away. How many times have I told you not to come up to the ranch every day. We don't want you here all the time. You are messing up our life. Do you hear that?

Brett (*patient; patronizing*) Lorenzo asked me to listen to the story.

Lawrence has already started off. Frieda goes after him and grabs his arm

Frieda Is that true? You asked her?

Lawrence (*shaking her off*) Stop being such a virago. It doesn't *matter*, all this.

Frieda It matters to me!

Brett goes off

Lawrence goes, pursued by Frieda, who is shouting as she goes

You said it would be good to have the Brett with us in America. She will stand between us and the world like a buffer you said. What she wants is to stand between you and me. She wants to be the little Jane Eyre to your Rochester. So who am I then? The mad hyena of a Mrs Rochester—that's who I have to be!

As her voice ceases, Student I starts to speak as if continuing a speech already begun. Solemn, a touch complacent, humourless; as are they all

Student I ... of the climate of that literary period and the effect of censorship, bad reviews and banning of the books on Lawrence's attitudes and style both in his life and in his writing. I posit a direct relationship between the adverse criticism of one work and the aggressive prose tone and more violent vocabulary contained in the work next written. This is not to imply that there is any shift toward pornography. The concensus in present-day Lawrentian scholarship is that in no sense does the work embody that kind of exploitative intention.

Professor (*nodding agreement*) I take it you include a statistical review.

Student I Of course.

Professor We may be able to make some useful connections here with the study on (*indicating Student III*) female influences and feminist elements.

Student III (*doubtfully*) I don't know ... My paper centres on content. I'm not really concerned with style except insofar as it may indicate bias or denial. I am interested in motivational factors. For example, Mabel Evans Dodge Sterne Luhan is the model for *The Woman Who Rode Away*. Is this because her fourth husband was a North American Indian?—bearing in mind that her former husbands were all wealthy, cultivated and cauca-sian. Also, was Lawrence aware that the Honourable Dorothy Brett's father, Viscount Esher, was a closet gay? Is there a cross connection with his own sexuality? Did he——?

Student IV Oh. Could I ask if this means you're touching on the homosex-ual aspects in the work and the life?

Student III Yes I am. Up to a point. The final section of my paper is subtitled "Lawrence's Sexual Ambivalence".

Professor (*to Student IV*) Is there an overlap with your project?

Student IV No no, it's just that I've done some quite extensive reading around in that area. (*To Student III*) Very interesting paper by Digworth—*Wounded Eros*. Did you happen to——?

Student III (*crisply*) I've read it. I thought the references were unreliable.

Student IV Oh I don't think so. As a matter of fact he——

Professor (*intervening*) Could I just check? (*To Student IV*) Your main emphasis is on the effects of Lawrence's tubercular condition?

Student IV Right. (*Instant lecture*) It's interesting that so many scholars describe the Lawrences as nomadic. It is true that from nineteen twelve when they ran away together until nineteen twenty-two when they first came here they lived in at least fifteen different places and countries but——

Student I (*with courteous scepticism*) Fifteen?

Student IV (*briskly*) Munich, Lerici, Lake Garda, London, Cornwall, Buckinghamshire, Berkshire, Derbyshire, Sussex, Capri, Taormina, Tuscany, Baden Baden, Ceylon and Australia. (*Brief pause. Then he resumes*) What isn't often pointed out is that Lawrence was searching not so much for new experiences and inspiration but for a location and climate that would be kind to what he always called his bronchials. In fact the extremes of climate here and in old Mexico were too severe for his health.

Professor Now on the question of old Mexico (*to Student II*) you're covering the two long stay periods there and the books from those periods, yes?

Student II Yes but my overall interest is in Lawrence as prophet and the religious resonances generally. I'd like to mention that although quite a lot of the writing from nineteen twenty-two to twenty-five is explicitly set in old Mexico, the internal evidence sometimes shows us he was describing the landscape around here. For instance, the cave described in the sacrifice section of *The Woman Who Rode Away* is actually only a few miles away from this ranch.

Professor (*again nodding agreement*) Now to sum up on this Intro-Discussion, I'd like to emphasize that what we want from all of you is new information, new insights, new speculations and theories. We have to bear in mind that (one) Lawrence wrote eleven novels, seven plays, three travel books, forty-seven short stories, five volumes of poetry, several dozen essays and reviews and at least five thousand letters and that (two) since his death there have been over three hundred books written about him as well as literally countless articles and scholarly papers—not to speak of the *D. H. Lawrence Review* which is published quarterly in Delaware.

At some point during the last couple of speeches, there is the sound off-stage of a horse galloping in the distance. It gets closer and louder but no-one takes any notice of it. By now the sound is quite loud

Student I (*slightly patronizing*) I would say that we're all cognisant of the volume of the original work and the critical material but there is the whole question of . . . (*He stops. Puzzled, he tilts his head and listens*)

Professor Question of what?

Student I Can you hear something? (*He stands, nervous and apprehensive*)
Professor (*listening*) No, I don't think so.

*The other Students also shake their heads and say they can't hear anything but
by this time the sound is so loud we can't actually hear them. Then it stops
abruptly*

Lawrence enters. He stands for a moment, looking off

The Professor and the Students freeze

Lawrence (*shouting*) Frieda!

Frieda enters, dressed in a divided skirt, a buckskin jacket and a cowboy hat

Lawrence goes to her and hugs her

(*In a broad accent*) Has ter had a good ride then, lass?
Frieda Oh that Azul . . . he's such an excitable horse.
Lawrence Did he bolt with thee again? Did he, my darlin'?
Frieda (*evasively*) Oh no, he was just a little bit frightened of a porcupine.
Lawrence And wast tha frightened too, my duckie? I'll lay tha was.
Frieda (*pulling away*) Of course I wasn't.
Lawrence (*affectionately; not in dialect*) Oh come on, Frieda. You're
terrified of that great horse. Look how you talk to him all the time. (*He
mimics her accent*) "Not too fast now, my Azul . . . gently gently, Azul . . .
oh good Azul, brave Azul." It's just to hide how frightened you are.
Frieda (*pouting*) That isn't true, Lorenzo, I——

Lawrence kisses Frieda and then they smile at each other

Well . . . maybe a little bit. But I love riding him, I do really. He's such a
beautiful horse. Azul, the blue! (*Sensuously*) It's wonderful to feel his
great thighs moving, his powerful legs.
Lawrence (*with a shout of laughter*) Rubbish Frieda, you don't feel anything
of the sort. You've been reading my books.
Frieda (*petulantly*) You do nothing but mock me, Lawrence.

*Lawrence laughs and puts his arms around Frieda. He punctuates the
following with little kisses on her cheek and neck*

Lawrence (*in dialect*) Dinna fret now, my lass. Dinna be mardy, eh? Eh?
(*Smoothing back her hair*) Look at thee all blown about. Th'art a mucky
little hussy, 'appen tha art. Eh my beauty? Eh my pigeon?

*Frieda laughs delightedly and puts her arms around Lawrence. They stand
peacefully entwined*

Lawrence (*sighing; not in dialect*) Oh I wish we hadn't told Mabel we'd go
down there tonight.
Frieda It's only for the evening. She'll give us a lovely delicious supper. And
Bynner and the Spoodle will be there. We can play charades.
Lawrence (*impatiently*) Oh well yes . . . yes. (*He breaks away from Frieda*)
He doesn't really like you to call him Spoodle, you know.

Frieda Oh all right, Spud, then. Ach so American. Spud Johnson. The fresh-face-small-town-boy name. But I like him. Well, I like them both. And Hal Bynner is a good poet I say, no matter what you think.

Lawrence Poet? How could anyone be a poet with a name like that? Witter Bynner. Witter witter witter—that's what he does in those poems of his.

Frieda You're just being narrow-minded and English and what do you call that? Jingoistic.

Lawrence (*outraged*) I? Jingoistic? I who have been persecuted and repudiated by my country, who——

Frieda Yes. You are. He is not English, he has a funny not-English name so he is no good as a poet. That's what you think. Anyway he likes to be called Hal. (*She laughs*) They are a charming couple—Hal Bynner the husband, ja? And Spoodle the good little wife.

Lawrence (*annoyed and fastidious*) Frieda, they are simply friends who happen to share a house. There is no couple about it. Why you always——

Frieda (*delighted*) Ah! The great D. H. Lawrence, the prophet of freedom and love and passion . . . so nervous of a couple of nice little American buggers.

Lawrence (*shrilly*) Don't be disgusting, Frieda. Stop it.

Frieda (*soothing*) OK I stop, I stop. I'm only teasing you. Is the Brett up here or down at her place?

Lawrence She's here, making some tea. Be nice to her. She hasn't been up to see us for three days.

Frieda (*injured*) I am nice to her. We're going to go blackberrying tomorrow. I have arranged it. But it is true, Lorenzo, admit it. It was much nicer the first year when we came here—without Brett.

Lawrence I don't know about nicer so much. There was all that fuss about Mabel's book. You were always shouting at her.

Frieda (*placidly*) Oh I wasn't. Anyway you only wanted Brett to come because her father is Viscount Esher. You're such a snob.

Lawrence I'm not a snob! I wanted all of them to come, not just Brett. Murry and Gertler and Koteliansky—all of them.

Frieda You and your Rananim. Well only the Brett did come. And that was just because you were her latest great romantic, obsessive infatuation.

Lawrence (*irritated*) Frieda, if you're going to——

Frieda Anyhow you are a snob. Who wrote all his letters on *my* papa's notepaper—because of the baronial crest. (*She nods, smiling*) Ja. Ja.

Lawrence Rubbish. I was just using that paper up. Come on. Tea'll be ready by now.

Frieda But do we have time? What time is Mabel sending the car up for us?

Lawrence Six. I hope Tony will be there tonight. She's not so bad when he's there.

Frieda I think he's gone to Santa Fe.

Lawrence A little holiday from his white buffalo.

Frieda (*laughing*) I like the way he is always so silent. He stands there, (*She takes up an Indian brave posture, arms crossed*) "Yes. No. OK." And Mabel talks and talks like a waterfall and he is like a rock in the middle of all those rushing words. That's what you'd like me to do, wouldn't you, Lorenzo. Yes. No. OK.

Lawrence (*delighted*) What a fool you are, Frieda. (*He takes her hand and they start off*) I've decided to have a phoenix on the cover of this new book. I think it'll be my symbol. I made a lovely drawing of one today. I'll show you.

Frieda Well if you're the phoenix, what am I?

Lawrence The nest of course.

Frieda Oh yes? Well if I'm the nest you'll be sitting on thorns, Mister.

Frieda and Lawrence laugh

Ach, Lawrence, do you know the very first time I saw you, when you walked so fast and light into our house I said to myself, "What kind of a bird is this?"

Black-out except for a light on Student I who stands, facing the audience. The Professor and the other students are sitting facing up to him. Student I gives the impression that he is just going on talking. He talks all the way through the following sequence but much of the time (as indicated) he is inaudible

Student I ... and certainly, second only to his mother, the most important influence in his whole life. Born in Austria, the Baroness von Richthofen—her first cousin was the famous flying ace, the Red Baron of World War I—she had married a professor from Nottingham who had come to holiday in Austria when she was eighteen. He, Ernest Weekly, was fifteen years older. They had three children and lived in a comfortable middle-class district of Nottingham. In nineteen eleven Lawrence's mother died of cancer and he became profoundly depressed and run-down and nearly died himself of pneumonia. In nineteen twelve he decided to go and work in Germany. Thank you.

A square of light comes up on Lawrence and Frieda standing looking at each other, their right hands linked

He had studied at Nottingham University with Ernest Weekly when he was a student and ... (*He goes on talking but in an inaudible murmur*)

Frieda (*shaking Lawrence's hand*) Mr Lawrence.

Lawrence Professor Weekly asked me to lunch.

Frieda He told me you were coming. He says you are one of the best of his students.

Lawrence Was. I've been a schoolmaster in London for two years.

Frieda (*looking right at him*) Do you enjoy that?

Lawrence gets locked into Frieda's look. There is a longish pause

Lawrence I ... sorry, what did you say?

Student I Next.

Black-out, and the sound of a slide being changed. The square of light comes up again

This was a very different and new experience for him. The crucial oedipal relationship with his mother, the intellectual almost literary love affair with Jessie Chambers, the purely sexual experience with Alice Dax but nothing like this. Frieda Weekly was a very passionate woman. She was sexually disappointed in her marriage and had already had one or two minor adulterous adventures. Not long after she and Lawrence ... (*He reverts to the inaudible murmur*)

In the square of light Lawrence and Frieda stand very close to each other still looking into each other's eyes

Frieda My husband is away tonight. Will you stay with me?
Lawrence (*shocked*) No. Not in his house. We must go away together.
Frieda (*beaming at him*) OK. I am going to Germany to visit my parents next week. You could come over too and stay in a hotel in the town.
Student I Next.

Black-out. Slide change sound. The square of light comes up on Frieda standing with Lawrence kneeling in front of her, his arms around her

She came nearly every day to his little attic hotel room in the town of Metz from her family's house and they made love. For Lawrence this was ... (*He goes back to murmuring*)

Lawrence gets up and kisses Frieda passionately

Lawrence (*ecstatically*) Never never could I have conceived what love was. The world is wonderful and beautiful and good. I shall love you all my life.
Frieda (*laughing with happiness*) And I will too.
Lawrence I've written to your husband.
Frieda (*pulling away, frightened*) Ach Lawrence—what did you say to him?
Lawrence I told him we loved each other. I told him I knew how terrible all this would be for him but that we were all suffering. I told him you would have to leave him.
Frieda But my children, Lawrence, my children!
Lawrence Oh he'll understand that the children should be with you. I'll make a better life for you and your children, Frieda, I promise you.
Student I Next.

Black-out. Slide change. The Lights come up on Frieda prostrate on the floor. Lawrence is crouched beside her

The boy was thirteen and the two girls ten and eight and she loved them passionately. Her husband wrote to her that she could never see them again. Now began the ... (*He reverts to murmuring again*)

Frieda raises herself up and looks imploringly at Lawrence

Frieda (*weeping*) What kind of an unnatural mother would I be if I didn't weep? He won't let them write to me, he intercepts my letters to them ... I know he tells them I am a wicked monster of a woman and tries to make them hate me. (*She weeps harder*) I can't bear it, I can't bear it.

Lawrence Don't you love me then, Frieda? Aren't you happy with me?
Frieda You know I am. I've never loved anybody the way I love you. But I
love them too. I'm being torn to pieces.
Lawrence (*standing up; angrily*) Leave me, then! Leave me and go back to
England and those brats of yours!
Student I Next.

*Black-out. Slide change. The Lights come up on Lawrence sitting on the floor,
knees up, miming writing in a notebook. Frieda sits next to him, her arm
around his shoulder. They hold this during the next speech*

And on through Austria to Italy like a honeymoon, wandering through
the Alps laughing and singing and making love, sleeping in haystacks and
living off new laid eggs, goats' cheese, strawberries and wine. All this is
described in his verse sequence, *Look! We have come through!* But the bliss
and happiness alternated with violent stormy scenes about Frieda's
children. And all the time Lawrence was writing. At that time he was . . .
(*He reverts to murmuring*)

Lawrence reads from the notebook to Frieda

Lawrence "He shook hands and left her at the door of her cousin's house.
When he turned away he felt the last hold for him had gone. The town
stretched away . . . beyond the town the country, little smouldering spots
for more towns—the sea—the night—and on and on! And he had no
place in it. Whatever spot he stood on, there he stood alone. From his
breast, from his mouth, sprang the endless space and it was there behind
him, everywhere. The people hurrying along the streets offered no
obstruction to the void in which he found himself. Everywhere the
vastness and terror of the immense night which is roused and stirred for a
brief while by the day, but which returns and will remain at last eternal,
holding everything in its silence. There was no time only space. Who
could say his mother had lived and did not live? She had been in one place
and was in another; that was all. And his soul could not leave her,
wherever she was. Now she had gone abroad into the night and he . . ."
(*He breaks off*) Oh Frieda, it's too hard to write all this.
Frieda But you must write it, Lorenzo, you must. It is good to get all this
out and into the book. Then you can be free from this suffocating love for
her.
Lawrence Don't start on all those theories of yours again.
Frieda But it's true, Lorenzo, you know that. You say it yourself in this
book. Here . . . (*She takes the notebook and flips through the pages*) Look,
this place—after she dies and the sister comes to tell him. (*She reads*)
"Annie came flying across the yard, half crying, half mad. 'Paul . . . Paul
. . . she's gone.' In a second he was in the house and upstairs. She lay
curled up and still, with her face on her hand, and nurse was wiping her
mouth. They all stood back. He kneeled down and put his face to hers and
his arms around her. 'My love—my love—oh my love,' he whispered
again and again. 'My love—oh my love.'"

During the last part of this Lawrence has hidden his face in his hands

(*Putting her arms around Lawrence*) She *was* your love and you couldn't
be free to love any other woman until she was dead.

Lawrence (*his head against Frieda's breast*) I know. Yes I know.

Frieda But now you have me. Now I am your love.

Student I Next.

*Black-out. Slide change. The Light come up on Lawrence and Frieda standing
facing out.* Lawrence *is in the act of putting a ring on her finger*

In July nineteen thirteen Frieda had finally been given a divorce by Ernest
Weekly and the marriage took place in the Kensington Register Office.
John Middleton Murry and Katherine Mansfield were witnesses. And it
was that summer that Lawrence went on a walking tour of the Lake
District with his friend and . . . (*He goes back to murmuring*)

Lawrence (*turning to Frieda*) You could come too. Why don't you come
with Kot and me?

Frieda No, I wouldn't have a nice time. He doesn't like me, your Koteliansky. You go, Lorenzo.

Student I Next.

Black-out. Slide change

*The Lights come up on Mabel, wearing an Indian head-dress, and an Indian
blanket over her dress. She is smiling*

Oh I'm sorry. Wrong slide.

Black-out. Slide change

The Lights come up on Brett wearing a twenties' party dress. Black-out

No. That's right. That's right.

The Lights up again on Brett in the square of light

Student I That walking tour with Koteliansky led directly to the famous
night at the Café Royal in London some years later and the first
significant meeting with the Honourable Dorothy Brett. On two or three
previous occasions she had already met and . . . (*He reverts again to
murmuring*)

*Brett holds up a piece of notepaper, reads it to herself and clasps it to her
breast*

Brett Oh Lorenzo, I was so hoping that you'd invite me. Murry told me you
were giving a supper party. Mark Gertler will be there and Koteliansky
and Catherine and Mary Canaan—all of them. I was longing to be asked!
Murry says you told him it's a Rananim party. I've heard you talk so
beautifully and passionately about Rananim, Lorenzo. The little colony
of artists away from the sickness of civilization and war, the mechaniza-
tion and sterility and——

Student I Next.

Black-out. Slide change. The Lights come up on Lawrence facing out and Brett and Frieda on either side of him a little distance behind him

Many bottles of claret were drunk followed by port. Lawrence was in a very excited and exalted state. Koteliansky made a drunken speech praising Lawrence and smashed a lot of wine glasses. Lawrence himself was obviously . . .

Lawrence No, don't stop him. Smash them all, Kot, smash them all. (*He sways, smiling foolishly; then begins to sing very loudly*) Rananim sadekin badenoi . . . Rananim sadekin badenoi—do you remember teaching me that old Hebrew chant, Kot? Remember? On our walking tour (*laughing*) when it poured with rain. Those girls laughing at us because we were singing our heads off in the rain and I had those yellow water lilies tied around my hat, remember? (*He sings*) Rananim sadekin . . . (*He breaks off. Loudly; intensely*) And what does it mean? Eh? Eh? It means rejoice O ye righteous in the Lord! And the word re-ananim means green! Fresh! Flourishing! New shoots of life. New green shoots. That's what we'll be in Rananim!

Frieda (*from the darkness*) Sit down, Lawrence. You are the one who is green. He shouldn't have drunk that port. It's poison to him.

Brett (*from the darkness; lyrically*) Lorenzo crowned with golden lilies!

Lawrence (*aggressively*) No I won't sit down. I've got something to say! (*Slurred*) Oh my friends, I've known you all for such a long time, so many years. (*He sings*) Dear old pals, jolly old pals. Clinging together in all sorts of weather. (*Then very dramatically*) Will you leave everything and follow me? Will you come with me to New Mexico and start a new life? Our little world, our Rananim . . . our heaven on earth!

Brett (*from the darkness*) I'll come, Lorenzo. I'll follow you!

Frieda (*from the darkness; grimly*) Yes . . .

Lawrence (*incoherently; eyes closed*) Yes yes yes! We will all be together. It will come true, I know it will all come true. Rejoice O ye righteous in the Lord. Rejoice . . . rejoice . . . (*He falls forward*)

Black-out. The café music comes up loud and there is a babble of voices and over it the sound of Lawrence vomitting. Cut to silence

Lawrence, Frieda and Brett exit in the Black-out

Student I Lights please.

The Lights come up on the whole stage. Only the students and the Professor are there

That's the end of Part One. Part Two, which I'll show at the next session, is called *The American Adventure*.

Professor I think we should point out that the Café Royal incident we've just been discussing took place after the Lawrences had visited New Mexico the first time in nineteen twenty-two. An interesting point here is that Mabel Dodge Luhan's Pueblo Indian husband Tony, was not at all in favour of her inviting Lawrence here to write about his tribe. However, Mabel was a very strong-minded woman and as usual she got her——

He is interrupted by Lawrence shouting off-stage

Lawrence (*off*) Mabel!

Lawrence enters and stands among the Students and Professor who freeze

(*Even louder*) Mabel!

Mabel (*off, the other side of the stage*) Come on in, Lorenzo. I'm in the living-room.

Lawrence I don't want to come in. You come out. I want to talk to you.

Mabel comes out

Lawrence goes to Mabel. She's carrying a book

Mabel Lorenzo, you have got to read this book! Jung. Fascinating. I've been completely enthralled. I sat down two hours ago just to leaf through the book and I haven't moved! I have not moved.

Lawrence Mabel . . .

Mabel Oh I know what you'll say, Mabel's off on one of her crazy hobby horses again, but you're wrong. This man understands the soul, Lorenzo—the wonder and magic and mystery of the soul. I promise you when I'm reading it I feel he is talking to me, to me personally. It's simply miraculous the way he——

Lawrence Mabel . . .

Mabel There's a whole section on extrovert and introvert personalities. Stunning. You and I, Lorenzo, we *are* introverts. We are simply *described* here. The whole artistic thing—well the spiritual, psychic thing—it's so——

Lawrence Mabel! Frieda and I are leaving.

Mabel Leaving? What do you mean?

Lawrence We're going back to Europe.

Mabel What!

Lawrence It's no good, Mabel, we can't stay. Frieda and I have talked the whole thing over.

Mabel But you've only been here three months! I had that little adobe house built specially for you.

Lawrence (*defensively*) I pay rent for it.

Mabel There was no need. I didn't want you to.

Lawrence I hate being beholden.

Mabel But why do you have to leave? Why? (*With realization*) It's Frieda, isn't it. She's jealous of me.

Lawrence Not jealous. She knows she's no need of that.

Mabel (*dashed*) Oh.

Lawrence But she thinks we're better off on our own. We're all too close to each other here. In each other's pockets. And she doesn't want me writing that book with you.

Mabel (*scornfully*) Goodness, you don't have to tell me that! She's tried to stymie that every way she possibly could. We have to work at your place so she can hear everything we say and interrupt all the time. She reads all

the notes I send over to you no matter how personal they might be, she's
always telling me you've gone out when you haven't, she——
Lawrence It's not just Frieda. I'm sick of the battle of wills between you and
me. I won't be bossed about and I won't be owned.
Mabel (*indignantly*) I don't know what you mean.
Lawrence Oh yes you do. You want to run me, Mabel, and I won't have it.
The second day after we arrived here you packed me off to that Apache
festival . . . driving hundreds of miles and I detest motor cars. But no, no,
I must see it, I must write about it, I must do as you'd decided I'd do. And
you've been carrying on like that ever since. I won't be pushed and pulled
and organized and that's flat. We shall be leaving in a fortnight.
Mabel (*emotionally*) Oh Lorenzo, don't go, please don't go! I won't
organize you anymore, I promise.
Lawrence You will. You can't help yourself. No, we'd best be off.
Mabel Oh listen, listen, I've just had a wonderful idea. I'll give you the little
ranch.
Lawrence Little ranch?
Mabel You know, up in the foothills. The one Tony drove us up to the
other week and the car broke down on the way back. Kiowa ranch.
Lawrence Oh ay, I remember.
Mabel Well you can have it. A present from me.
Lawrence I thought you were giving it to your son.
Mabel Oh he won't mind. Take it, Lorenzo.

Lawrence pauses, then shakes his head

Lawrence No. I couldn't. I've no desire to own property. I hate all that.
Mabel I'll give it to Frieda, then. She'd take it.
Lawrence Well . . .
Mabel Oh please Lorenzo, let me. I can't bear it if you go. You'll see, it'll
work out beautifully. You will be on your own but we'll be able to visit
each other and you can take a couple of the horses up there . . . oh please
say yes.
Lawrence I'll speak to Frieda.
Mabel Wait. I'll go get the deeds. I've got them in my desk. Wait right there,
Lorenzo.

Mabel exits

*There is a light change. Lawrence walks downstage humming to himself and
gazing round*

Lawrence This ranch, this little Kiowa ranch. (*He looks out as into the
distance*) The desert . . . the mountains . . . There's something here that
loves me and wants me. It's a spirit. And it's here on this ranch. It's here
in this landscape. It's something big. Bigger than men, bigger than
religion, something to do with wild America. It's something wild that
hurts me sometimes and wears me down sometimes, I know that, but it
craves me, it needs me. There's a wild spirit here that wants me. And
everything I've ever written here, the novels, the poems, the stories about

this country and about Mexico, they're all full of that wild dark power . . . and they're all sad. Well after all, they're true to what is, to all the old old ghosts of this place. The ghosts of the Rocky Mountains, I know them, they know me, we go well together. Listen ghosts! I know that I am I. That my soul is a dark forest and that my known self will never be more than a little clearing in the forest. That gods, strange gods, come forth from the forest into the clearing of my known self and then go back. And I know that I will always try to recognize and submit to the gods in me and the gods in other men and women.

Frieda enters

Frieda Lorenzo.

Lawrence does not answer

The car's here, Lawrence. Didn't you hear me calling?
Lawrence What?
Frieda Mabel's car! Are you coming or aren't you?
Lawrence I'm coming, I'm coming!

Lawrence goes

Frieda follows him but Student IV starts to speak just before she leaves the stage

Student IV There is one thing I'd like to say . . .

Frieda turns back and goes to him at once

Frieda (*taking his arm*) Don't say it, Hal, I know, I know! You're always telling me I won't get anywhere with him about my children if I try and fight him but I can't help myself.
Student IV (*patting her hand*) Honestly, Frieda dear, I would have thought you'd have learned to use a bit of guile with Lorenzo after all these years.
Frieda But he's wrong and stupid and stubborn, Hal! Why shouldn't my own children come and stay with us here on my own ranch? It's so unfair.
Student IV Who ever said Lorenzo was fair? You have to handle him, Frieda. You're never going to batter him into submission.
Frieda (*laughing*) No? One time in Cornwall we had a big fight about my children. He thought he had the last word of course. (*She mimics*) We'll say no more about it, Frieda. He was always saying that, it made me so mad. And then he went off to wash the supper dishes—singing while he washed them! I came up behind him—bang crash! A big stoneware plate right on his head. You should have seen his face, he was amazed! I had the last word that night. Ja! (*She laughs but it turns to tears*) Oh Hal, he is so jealous of my children he wants me never to see them again.
Student IV Don't cry, Frieda, please don't be upset. Here come the others.

A set is flown or wheeled in to represent Mabel's living-room

Mabel, Lawrence and Brett come on carrying cushions, a dressing-up clothes box etc.

Mabel Oh here you are, you two. We've been looking all over for you. Spud said you . . . (*She looks around*) Spud? Drat. Now we've lost him.
Lawrence (*going to Student I*) Here he is. Come on, Spoodle. (*Taking him to join the others*) No slacking off, eh?
Mabel Honestly, we keep losing track of ourselves tonight. Put this over there, will you, Spud dear?
Spud Sure, Mabel. (*He glances at Frieda*) Are you OK, Frieda?
Lawrence (*edgily*) Yes. What's the matter with you for goodness' sake?
Frieda (*flustered, blowing her nose*) Nothing. I'm fine. I'm fine.
Mabel (*curiously*) You haven't been crying, have you?
Student IV I was reciting some of my poems to Frieda. She's paid me the compliment of saying they were moving.
Frieda (*nodding vigorously*) Ja. Ja. Beautiful.
Student I What ones did you recite to her, Hal?
Lawrence (*unpleasantly*) Yes Bynner, let us hear one of these affecting works. Recite one to us. We'd like to be moved too, wouldn't we, Brett?
Brett What?
Lawrence Oh nothing, nothing. Go on, Bynner.
Student IV No, I'll recite one of yours, shall I Lorenzo? (*He then recites with somewhat exaggerated dramatic feeling*)
    But the shadow of lying was in your eyes.
    The mother in you, fierce as a murdress, glaring to England,
    Yearning towards England, towards your young children
    Insisting upon your motherhood, devastating.
Brett (*beaming at Lawrence*) Beautiful.
Frieda (*nervously*) Oh come on Hal, we want to hear your own——
Student IV (*overriding*)   Lot's wife . . .! not wife, but mother.
    I have learned to curse your motherhood,
    You pillar of salt accursed.
    I have cursed motherhood because of you.
    Accursed, base motherhood!
Lawrence (*starting off, angrily*) I didn't come down here to be wittered at.
Mabel (*taking his arm*) Now now, Lorenzo, don't be so hot tempered.
Brett What's the matter? Recite some more, Hal, do.
Lawrence Leave me alone, Mabel!
Student I Hal, tell Lorenzo you were only——

Frieda interrupts

Frieda   Never mind,
    It is finished, the spring is here
    And we're going to be summer-happy
    And summer-kind.
    We have died, we have slain and been slain
    We are not our old selves anymore.
    I feel new and eager
    To start again.

Lawrence has watched Frieda expressionlessly. Now he smiles

Lawrence   And yet all the while you are you, you are not me.
　　　　　　And I am I, I am never you.
　　　　　　How awfully distinct and far off from each other's being we
　　　　　　　are!
　　　　　　Yet I am glad.
　　　　　　I am so glad there is always you beyond my scope,
　　　　　　Something that stands over,
　　　　　　Something I shall never be,
　　　　　　That I shall always wonder over and wait for,
　　　　　　Look for like the breath of life as long as I live,
　　　　　　Still waiting for you, however old you are, and I am,
　　　　　　I shall always wonder over you and look for you.

There is a pause. They stand silent, looking at each other and smiling

Brett (*plaintively*) I thought we were going to play Mah Jong.
Mabel Oh not Mah Jong again!
Student I Why don't we dance to the victrola?
Frieda Yes yes, let's dance. Ragtime! Come on, Spud. We'll go and get it.
Lawrence Dancing! You call this modern tail-wagging stuff dancing?
Frieda Oh Lorenzo don't be so stuffy.

Frieda exits with Student I

Mabel puts her arm around Student III

Mabel Oh you're back. (*She puts her other arm round Student II*) How did
you enjoy the Pueblo, Bessie?
Student II Simply amazing. Of course Ida's seen it before.
Student III It's like another world, isn't it?
Student IV Ida Rauh! I didn't know you'd arrived. (*He kisses her*) Bessie,
you didn't tell me Ida was coming.
Student II I didn't know. Mabel didn't tell me.
Lawrence I didn't know either of you were in Taos. (*He takes them both by
the hand*) Mrs Freeman—Ida. I'm that pleased to see you again.
Student II Oh, Bessie, please Lorenzo. You can't be more pleased than me.
I always love visiting Taos but especially when you're here.
Student III What about the play you promised to write for me, Lorenzo?
Lawrence (*laughing*) Now Ida lass, be patient.
Mabel Isn't this a nice surprise for you, Lorenzo? I know how you like to be
surrounded by adoring women.

She gets Brett and brings her over

(*Shouting*) This is Bessie Freeman. We grew up together in Buffalo, New
York. And Ida Rauh—she's on the stage. This is Dorothy Brett, well she's
really the Honourable Dorothy but we all just call her Brett, don't we?
Brett (*coolly*) Lorenzo calls me Brett, Frieda calls me *the* Brett and Mabel
doesn't often call me anything. I think she'd quite like me to disappear
altogether.
Mabel (*annoyed*) Oh nonsense.

Brett Look, there's Tony.
Mabel Where?

Brett points at the Professor. Everyone looks at him. He sits impassive and unaware

Brett (*after a pause*) How silly of me. There's nobody there.

Frieda enters with Student I who carries the victrola

Frieda Ach but who is here? How lovely. How nice. (*She kisses them*)
Student III Hi, Frieda darling, I love your dress.
Student I Ida how marvellous to see you. Evening Bessie, dear.
Frieda Just in time for some dancing. (*She puts a record on and starts it*)
Student II Oh I'm too old for dancing.
Student IV (*to Ida*) So how's Broadway?
Student III Don't tease. One summer stock job this year . . .
Frieda Spud, you dance with Ida, ja? You are such a good dancing couple together. I remember from last year. Like professionals you two.
Lawrence Nobody wants to dance, Frieda.
Frieda You mean you don't want to so nobody else must. Everybody does want to. Oh see, look. Even the Brett.

Brett is into a dance of her own, rather out of time and a bit langourous

Lawrence (*bad-tempered*) Well if you all want to make idiots of yourselves. Bessie, come and sit down over here away from that dreadful racket.

Lawrence and Student II go and sit

Frieda (*clapping her hands*) Hal, will you dance with me?
Student IV With the very greatest pleasure, Baroness.

Ida and Student I are performing quite an intricate dance. All the latest steps

Frieda Now nothing fast and fancy like that, Hal.
Student IV (*as they start dancing*) Don't worry. I'm a terrible dancer.
Frieda You're too modest. You are a wonderful stately dignified dancer.
Student IV Flatterer. You and your honey tongue, Frieda.

Frieda laughs and kisses Student IV on the cheek. Lawrence sees this and scowls. Mabel goes up to Lawrence and bobs a playful curtsy

Mabel (*little girl flirtatious*) Come and dance with me, Lorenzo.
Lawrence (*curtly*) No thank you.
Mabel Pretty please?
Lawrence No! I don't want to dance with you or anybody else. Leave me alone, Mabel. (*Then to Student II*) When I think that we've seen Tony and his friends do their beautiful Indian dances in this very room! Form and ritual and power . . . and then look at that. (*He points at the dancers*). Jig jig jig, wiggle wiggle wiggle. It's a travesty.
Student II Oh Lorenzo, you're a terrible intolerant man.
Lawrence (*smiling at her*) I am.

Mabel goes and sits on a cushion, sulky. Brett comes downstage centre as she dances.

Brett (*to herself*) I'm dancing with you, Lorenzo. We hardly even touch each other but we move in perfect accord and we look deep into each others' eyes. You know so well how I feel about you. I'm positive you feel my silent waves of sympathy when Frieda is rough and selfish and noisy. You need peace and calm. You work so hard. My greatest joy is just sitting near you when you write. Mabel and Frieda both want to dominate you. They don't understand that what you need is gentleness. Oh Lorenzo, all I want is to be by your side always, watching over you.

Student IV twirls Frieda around. She laughs with pleasure

Student II Don't they make a handsome couple? She's such a beautiful woman, your wife.

Lawrence (*vituperatively*) She's a stupid fat fool!

In a sudden rush Lawrence gets up, goes and seizes Brett and dances her over to Student IV and Frieda and bumps into them hard. Mabel laughs. Brett cries out

Frieda Lawrence!
Student IV Ouch! Hey Lorenzo, watch out where you're going.
Lawrence (*elaborately apologetic*) Oh sorry sorry, so sorry. Do excuse us. Be more careful, Brett. Mind what you're doing.
Brett (*breathlessly*) Sorry, Lorenzo.

Lawrence dances Brett around and then again steers her over to Student IV and Frieda and bumps into them. Everyone stops dancing except Lawrence and Brett. Frieda stalks over to the gramophone and lifts the needle. Lawrence stops dancing, lets go of Brett and walks back to his chair

Lawrence (*as he goes*) Oh, is the dancing over? What a pity.

Lawrence sits down, crosses his legs and smiles affably. Frieda makes a furious noise and turns her back

Mabel (*to nobody in particular, crossly*) There now. The evening's ruined and it's all Frieda's fault.
Brett (*dreamily, to nobody*) Lorenzo and I danced. He always says he hates dancing but he danced with me.

The Professor and the four Students start moving slowly out of the room and returning to their real selves

The Professor exits

Lawrence suddenly uncrosses his legs and stands up, beaming. As he speaks the Students stop

Lawrence I know! We'll have charades.
Frieda No. (*But she turns around*)
Mabel Well . . .

Brett What, Lorenzo?

As Lawrence talks the Students are drawn in again

Lawrence Ida, I shall want you on my team. You too Spoodle. Give us a hand with this box. (*He drags out the dressing-up box*) Mabel, you can organize the other team.

Mabel (*petulantly*) Well really, Lorenzo, I don't see why we all have to——

Lawrence (*interrupting*) You can have Bynner on yours. Clear us an acting space, Hal, will you? Oh and Bessie, we'll need those cushions set out for the audience. Brett!

Brett (*blissfully moving toward Lawrence ready to dance again*) Here I am, Lorenzo.

Lawrence turns Brett round and pushes her to Mabel

Lawrence You're on Mabel's team.

Brett (*confused*) Team? What? What's happening?

Mabel (*shouting irritably into her ear trumpet*) Charades!

Brett Oh. Right oh, Lorenzo.

Lawrence Now then Bessie, you're on my team too.

Student II Oh my goodness, I can't act.

Lawrence Rubbish. You're another, Duse, you know you are. Now, Frieda . . .

Frieda Don't you now Frieda me. Look at you, bossing everybody all over the place. You say nobody wants to dance. I say nobody wants to play charades.

Lawrence (*friendly*) Don't be silly, Frieda, of course they do. Mabel wants to and she's our hostess.

Frieda No she doesn't.

Mabel (*promptly*) Yes I do.

Lawrence You see? And how you can possibly call me bossy? Hal, I appeal to you. Am I a bossy man?

Student IV You, Lorenzo? I never knew a milder-mannered fellow in my life.

Student III Always so meek and gentle.

Student II A regular shrinking violet.

Student I I'll tell the world!

Everyone laughs, Frieda reluctantly joining in

Lawrence There now. Off you go, Frieda. You're on Mabel's team. We'll go first because I've thought of a very good word. Mabel, you people can think up yours while we get ready.

Mabel (*with a mock salute; whimsically*) Ay, ay, sir!

Mabel and Frieda and Brett and Student IV get into a group and talk. Lawrence is getting out costumes and instructing his team

Brett (*excitedly*) Oh listen! I've got a lovely one. (*She whispers*)

Mabel Oh really! I never heard anything so dumb.

Student IV (*tactfully*) I don't see how we'd act it.

Brett (*putting her hands up and hopping about*) Well I thought one of us could——

Frieda (*scathing*) Kangaroo! Anyway he would guess it straight away. You're so silly, Brett.

Brett (*taking umbrage*) Oh sorry I spoke, I'm sure.

Student IV Now, ladies . . . we'll just have to think of another one.

Mabel (*calling across*) It isn't fair, Lorenzo. Poor Hal's our only man.

Lawrence (*maliciously*) I want to see if Bynner can stand up to you three better than I do.

Student II (*to Lawrence*) You still haven't told me what to do. I really can't act, I promise you.

Lawrence whispers to Student II

Oh, you wicked thing. Well, I'll try.

Student IV No no, that won't work, Mabel. It's much too complicated. Wait a minute, wait a minute, how about this?

Student IV and Mabel put their heads together again

Frieda Perfect! Lovely!

Lawrence We're ready. First syllable.

The others settle themselves to watch. Lawrence has put on a dress and a ribbon around his head that makes him look like Mabel. He mimes dusting things with a feather duster. He speaks with a terrible American accent

Oh I'm such a collector. I've collected so much it seems silly not to open a shop and sell some of it. (*He sings as he dusts*) "Buffalo girls won't you come out tonight, come out tonight, come out—"

Student III walks toward Lawrence in an Indian blanket and head-dress

Well hello. Come on in. What do you want to buy?

Student III Me want new blanket.

Lawrence Oh I don't have anything like that. I don't sell useful things for heaven's sake. I sell art! I know! What about a set of my memoirs—all five volumes. (*He mimes offering heavy stack of books*)

Student III Me no want.

Lawrence You'll be sorry one day, believe me. Well maybe you'd like a nice painting to put up in your tepee. Hundreds of artists come to see me you know and they always give me their pictures. Here's some desert pictures and some forest pictures and some Indian pictures—wouldn't you like one of those?

Student III Me no want.

Lawrence Oh I know the perfect thing. Look at this. It's a portrait of a genius.

Lawrence mimes holding up a picture to Student III who backs away alarmed

Student III That red-beard-loud-shouter-crazy-man!

Lawrence I'm selling him very cheap.

Student III (*running away*) Me no want!

Student I approaches as a ragged drunk

Student I Hey girlie, will you sell me something?
Lawrence Are you an artist?
Student I No I'm a bum. (*Pause*) Hallelujah.
Lawrence I'm sorry but I only serve artists—and our wonderful, poetical, romantic red Indians of course.
Student I All I want is some moonshine. You got a little hooch?
Lawrence No I do not. Get out.
Student I Oh come on. Isn't this a haberdasher? Haberdasher rum—haberdasher whiskey? Sell me some whiskey.
Lawrence I wouldn't sell you the wax out of my ears. Get out of here you untalented unimportant person. A prison cell is where you ought to be. Out! Out! Out!

Lawrence chases Student I off and then returns, taking off the ribbon

That's the end of that bit.
Mabel (*huffily*) There's such a thing as getting too personal you know.
Frieda (*who has laughed heartily throughout*) Oh, Mabel.
Student IV Be a sport now, Mabel.
Mabel All I'm saying is——
Lawrence Second syllable. (*To Student II*) Off you go, Bessie.

Student II approaches wearing a cape and a hat. She keeps getting the giggles and she speaks with a very exaggerated German accent

Student II Oh I so loff zis rrrranch! Wunderbar! Ze beautiful wild animals, ze marvellous birds, ze fascinating snakes ... (*Looking down*) A snake! Eeeeeeeeee! (*Then with a glance at the other team*) Zet is all I can say ... Eeeeeeee! (*She curtsys, then speaks with her own accent*) The end.
Student IV (*laughing*) Priceless, Bessie!

Student II blows an apologetic kiss to Frieda. Mabel is laughing delightedly

Frieda (*laughing*) But I love snakes!
Brett What was she saying? I couldn't understand a word of it.
Mabel Not *now*, Brett.

Student III approaches dressed to look like Brett. She mimes sitting on a bank and fishing. Student I comes up to her wearing a red beard

Student III (*without looking around*) Hello.
Student I (*in a terrible North-Country accent*) By goom, how did you know I were there, lass?
Student III Oh I always know where you are and wherever that is I'll be there.

Mabel and Frieda laugh. Brett looks perplexed

Student I Fishing are you?
Student III (*miming an ear trumpet*) What?
Student I I said were you fishing?

Student III Oh you're so amazing. You never have to be told what a person's doing. You just know by your wonderful intuitions and sensitivity.

Student I Well I am a genius you know, lass. What's that tha'rt using for bait, eh?

Student III Little pieces of my heart. I thought the fishes might as well have it if nobody else wanted it.

Student I Well I'll go to our house! Eee, but that's a daft notion, that is. A heart for bait.

Students I and III stand up and bow. Applause

Brett (*revelation*) I think she was being me!

Everyone laughs. Lawrence claps his hands for attention

Lawrence Whole word!

Lawrence and Student I have put on clergyman's dog collars and walk around arm in arm

Lawrence So this is Mabeltown. Dear me, Vicar, all these houses appear to be made of mud.

Student I That's right, Reverend. Adobe we call it.

Lawrence I understand there's a Queen Mabel, Vicar.

Student I You bet your life, Reverend.

Lawrence Is it true that she eats painters for breakfast, poets for lunch and novelists for tea?

Mabel (*pouting but pleased*) Oh Lorenzo, there you go being mean to me again!

Brett (*with glee*) Queen Mabel.

Student II approaches, dressed as a tart

Lawrence But what have we here, Vicar?

Student I Oh that's just a townsperson I guess.

Lawrence Good-afternoon, townsperson.

Student III (*stroking Lawrence*) You're cute. You want to come and see where I live?

Lawrence How very kind. Delighted.

Student I No no, Reverend. What she means is . . . (*He whispers*)

Lawrence What? A scarlet woman? Leave me alone you abominable townsperson.

Student I Don't you understand? We don't do things like that.

Lawrence Never never never!

Now Student II joins them and they all take a bow together

Frieda Wonderful!

Student IV Spud, I never knew you could do a North-Country accent.

Lawrence He can't.

Mabel And wasn't Ida the perfect Brett!

Brett What? Celibate.

Lawrence (*laughing*) She's got it.
Frieda Got what?
Student I The word. Celibate!
Student IV Oh of course!
Frieda (*innocently*) Well it is a word she would guess, no?
Mabel (*laughing*) Frieda!
Student IV OK, girls, it's our turn now. Come on, Brett.

Lawrence and his team go and sit down on the cushions as the others make for the dressing-up box

Brett What? Oh well Lorenzo was selling things in the first part, you see—that's the cel part, then there was Bessie doing her——
Mabel We all know now, Brett.
Frieda (*friendly*) Do shut up. We're going to do ours now.
Brett Oh dear, are we? I've forgotten the word.
Student IV (*softly to her*) Diversion.
Brett Oh yes.

Frieda has got herself a homberg and a black doctor's bag. She stands to one side. Student IV lies down and covers himself with a blanket. Mabel and Brett, wearing shawls, go and kneel beside him

Lawrence and the Students are laughing and talking. Mabel and Brett shush them

Brett (*with exaggerated concern*) I think he's asleep.
Mabel (*melodramatically*) Yes. Thank God he's getting some rest.

A silence. Then Student IV starts to cough. The two women lift him up to a sitting position. The paroxysm of coughing stops

Brett Are you better now?
Student IV (*very loudly*) No!

The Lights change to a pool of light on Student IV. The two women sit back and bow their heads. Frieda is in the shadows behind them

I must have a temperature. (*Frantic and panicky*) I'm delirious. Give me the thermometer. Don't cry! (*He starts to pant*) Get the doctor. I ought to have some morphine now. (*Then terrified*) Hold me! Hold me! I don't know where I am. I don't know where my hands are. Where am I?
Frieda (*very loudly*) No!

Frieda throws off the hat and the bag and runs over to Student IV, pushing Brett and Mabel out of the way. She puts her arms around him and his head drops on her breast and his eyes close

The Lights fade slowly to black on the sound of her weeping

Oh my love, my love . . . oh my love.

CURTAIN

ACT II

The Lights come up on the ranch

*There is a divan in the house area on which Frieda lies smoking and reading.
Lawrence is sitting on the front porch sewing. The four Students are sitting
about and in and around the house. The Professor is sitting downstage on the
chair we saw in Act I. The following speeches come over as oddly disjointed,
both aggressive and confused. They speak not quite to themselves and not quite
to each other*

Student I An essentially puritanical man, he saw sex as sacred and marriage
as the most profoundly important relationship in life. He detested
pornography. Quote. "Pornography is the attempt to insult sex, to do dirt
on it. Pornographic books are either so ugly they'll make you ill or so
fatuous you can't imagine anybody but a cretin or a moron reading or
writing them. Only a natural fresh openness about sex will do any good
now. Without secrecy there would be no pornography." Close quote.

Student II Did the religious and moralistic aspects of the work reflect
Lawrence's actual attitudes in his own life? Has he been wrongly
interpreted as an exponent of free love? Would Lawrence have supported
Gay Liberation? (*Pause*) And related questions.

Student III Lawrence as anti-feminist. He repeatedly expressed the belief in
the necessary submission of women to men. He disapproved of women in
politics and often mocked career women. This suggests a possible and
fundamental fear of women——

*The sound off-stage in the distance of a gunshot. Student III stops speaking but
neither she nor anyone else on stage seems aware of the sound. After a pause
she simply continues as if she hadn't stopped*

—which might have its roots in his very early life when he saw that his
refined schoolteacher mother had little but contempt for his drunken,
coal-miner father.

Student IV The relationship between Lawrence's chronic tubercular condition and his supposed sexual impotence in the last few years of his life. An
interesting sidelight here is that much of his writing in those years was
preoccupied with sexual matters e.g. *Lady Chatterley's Lover*, the banned
poems, pansies, et cetera, et cetera.

Professor The unique value of being in residence on this ranch where he
himself lived and wrote, even if only for a few days, cannot really be

measured. Certainly it informs and enriches the group discussions and while we analyse the work we are also able to understand the man and of course the subsidiary characters of this period, the women who——(*He breaks off*)

Brett enters, carrying a gun, a dead rabbit and a bag over her shoulder. As she comes on the Professor and the Students freeze

Brett Cooee, Lorenzo!

Lawrence looks up, waves and goes back to his sewing. Brett goes up to him and gets out her ear trumpet

What are you sewing?

Lawrence Mending Frieda's jacket.

Brett Your sewing is so neat. Beautiful lit-tle lit-tle stitches. I couldn't sew like that.

Lawrence I daresay. Frieda certainly couldn't.

Brett (*complacently*) I'm afraid Frieda never learned to be much of a housewife, did she? You do everything—the cooking, the cleaning——

Lawrence Frieda washes the clothes. And she cooks sometimes—well, she likes making cakes. But she was brought up with servants, remember. We all had to turn to in our house, girls and boys both. My brothers and I could fettle and tidy as well as any woman when we were only bits of lads ... (*He breaks off*) You oughtn't to be here you know, Brett. You came up yesterday. Frieda will——

Brett Frieda's getting too bossy about what I do and don't do. I moved down to the Hawk's ranch when she said she didn't want me living in the cabin up here, didn't I? Wasn't that enough?

Lawrence Now Brett, you know we——

Brett And now she says I'm only to come up three days a week. She says. She says. I came to America because you asked me to, Lorenzo.

Lawrence (*putting down the sewing*) You stir up trouble, Brett. You do, you know. All these rows. It's very wearying for me. Frieda hates you, you know that, so can't you just——

Brett (*genuinely surprised*) Frieda doesn't hate me. I'm one of the best friends she's got.

Lawrence Really, Brett, can you be that dense? Of course she hates you. What do you think all our quarrels are about?

Brett (*even more surprised*) But you and Frieda always quarrel, Lorenzo, you always have. You're famous all over the world for your quarrels. Why should I think it was about me?

Lawrence (*looking at Brett for a moment*) I think you really didn't know. I thought you provoked her on purpose.

Brett (*round-eyed*) I wouldn't ever do anything to provoke Frieda, Lorenzo. Truly.

Lawrence Well, we'll say no more about it. (*He goes back to his sewing*) Did you know Mabel and Tony were here?

Brett No, when did they come up?

Lawrence This afternoon. They brought some of the other Indians with them. They've set up their tepees in the wood. Mabel wanted us to go and eat with them tonight but I told Frieda to say no.

Inside, Frieda has become aware of their voices, stopped reading and is raised up on one elbow listening, the cigarette hanging out of her mouth

Brett Good. I brought the painting to show you. I finished it. (*She gets a canvas out of her bag*) See? You writing under your favourite pine tree.

Lawrence (*laughing*) Well it's a very good likeness of the tree, Brett.

Brett (*laughing too*) I think I've done you beautifully. And look—I've brought supper as well.

Brett holds up the rabbit. Inside, Frieda has got up off the divan, thrown the book angrily down and gone to the porch door. She opens it

Frieda Brett! I knew it was you. What are you——? (*Then in amazement*) You got a rabbit! Did you shoot it yourself?

Brett (*pleased*) Yes.

Frieda (*very amused*) Well never in a hundred million years would I believe it. All those times—off you go with your gun but you never never catch anything. Good, Brett! *Brava!* But how will we skin it?

Lawrence I'll do it. (*Then irritably*) Take that filthy cigarette out of your mouth.

Frieda (*amiably*) No. I have been reading some short stories by James Joyce. Have you read *Ulysses*, Brett? It's a wonderful book.

Lawrence (*angrily*) The last part of it is dirty and indecent and obscene.

Frieda You wouldn't even read the end.

Lawrence Because it's filthy!

Frieda Oh you have to know best, naturally. You lay down the law as usual.

Brett I think Lorenzo's right. The last chapter is——

Frieda Of course you would think he is right, of course! You know, Brett, I would pay you half a crown if you would ever contradict Lawrence. Just once!

Brett What, Frieda? Sorry I didn't hear.

Frieda (*shouting*) I said——

Lawrence (*getting up*) I'm going to skin this rabbit. (*He gets up and then catches sight of the Professor*) Who left that there?

Frieda What?

Lawrence (*angrily*) This!

Lawrence grabs the chair and the Professor is catapulted suddenly to his feet. The Students stand up, alarmed

Student I Are you all right, sir?

The Professor, rooted and blank with astonishment, doesn't answer

Frieda I was sitting in it to do my painting of the horses this morning.

Student II (*to the Professor*) Is anything wrong?

Professor (*dazed*) No ... no ...

Lawrence (*banging the chair down*) You should have put it back on the porch when you'd finished.

The Professor walks distractedly toward the centre. He stares out front. The Students take an uncertain step or two toward him

Frieda (*angrily*) Well I wasn't finished, was I? You should know that!

Lawrence How many times have I told you not to leave this chair out? You know how quickly a cloudburst can come. All the decorations on this would be completely ruined.

Frieda All right! I'm sorry, I'm sorry!

Lawrence You're so sloppy and careless, Frieda. It's infuriating.

The Professor turns to face the Students

Professor (*with an effort*) Well . . .

Brett (*reproachfully*) Lorenzo made this chair himself, Frieda.

Frieda (*maddened*) I know he did. I know!

Professor (*looking at the Students without seeing them*) I think that just about finishes our . . . (*He trails off*) Yes . . . (*He starts out*) This session is . . . yes . . .

The Professor goes

The Students go off one by one, awkward and displaced and uneasy, during the following

Lawrence has picked up the rabbit and started into the house

Lawrence Did you remember to tell Mabel we wouldn't go up to their camp for supper?

Frieda (*sulkily*) Yes. I sent a message.

Lawrence Why didn't you tell her yourself?

Frieda Because I didn't want to go all the way up there. Why didn't you? I'm not just your errand boy, you know.

Lawrence makes an irritated sound and exits through the house

Brett (*sitting in the chair*) He loves this chair, Frieda.

Frieda He loves himself. Do you know what he did this morning? I was sitting there doing my picture of the corral when he came back from his writing. He wanted to see the painting and I said no he should wait till it was finished so he snatched it out of my hands and tore it into pieces and threw them on the ground. (*Near to tears*) Why does he act like that?

Brett (*with genuine friendliness*) I think it's because he gets so involved and emotional about his work.

Frieda I'm not used to playing second fiddle. Always at home I played first fiddle. I'm as important as Lawrence . . . he says so himself . . . but he always wants to be boss.

Brett (*with reproof*) He must have peace, you know, Frieda. He has a very great need to be cherished and——

Frieda (*angrily*) Oh by you, I suppose. You could protect him from the harsh world, couldn't you. And from me too you'd protect him! You and

Mabel, you're both alike. You think the worst mistake in his life was to marry me.

Brett No no ...

Frieda Yes yes! Oh yes, yes you do, ja! You think I am the loud stupid dummy who just gets in his way and spoils his life. You and Mabel and all your high falute. Well you should try sometime living with a genius and see how you like it!

Brett Frieda, I never said I——

Frieda You don't have to say anything. It's what you do. Running around behind him adoring him. Well maybe you would like it the times he flew into his rages and beat you, ja? You would like that? Look at this! (*She pulls up her skirt to show a bruise on her leg*) And this! (*She pulls down the shoulder of her blouse to show another*) He kicks me and he punches me— you think I'm so big and fat and strong but he's stronger than me I promise you. Is this what you and Mabel would——

Brett Honestly, there's no need to——

Frieda And I tell you something else. He couldn't do his writing without me. He has to have me there. He shows me everything he writes and he cares absolutely what I think. I must say yes to it, I must approve. You ask him, you and Mabel, ask him! (*She breaks off*) Anyway why are you up here today? You came up yesterday. This is my ranch and I won't have you here every day. And we said you should blow that whistle of yours when you get to the fence down there so we know you're coming but today here you are again, just——

Brett (*loudly*) Oh go to hell, Frieda!

Frieda (*taken aback*) What?

Brett I said go to hell. I have some rights. I know it's your ranch but remember I helped to build the kitchen and dig the well and mend the roof and paint the house and make the bread oven and——

Frieda I don't say you didn't work hard. You did. You do. (*Change of tack*) Shall I tell you what I hate the worst? You *love* Lawrence, oh how you love him and worship him, you have this great *schwarm* for him ... but you don't want to make love with him the way a real woman would. Believe me I would have more respect for you if you did. You are so——

Brett (*haughtily*) Really, Frieda, how could I make love to Lawrence when I am a guest? On *your* ranch.

Frieda (*with scorn*) Well anyway he would never never want to make love to a skinny asparagus stick like you.

Brett (*indignantly*) He's not all that fat himself, you know!

Frieda stares at her for a moment and then suddenly bursts out laughing. Then Brett laughs too

Frieda Oh Brett, Brett ... what a silly you are.

Mabel appears suddenly. She's obviously angry

Frieda and Brett stop laughing

Mabel (*coldly*) Where is Lorenzo?

Frieda In the kitchen.

Mabel Thank you.

Mabel walks past Frieda and Brett into the house

Brett and Frieda look at each other and then go quietly into the house to listen to the voices of Lawrence and Mabel off-stage in the kitchen

Mabel (*off*) May I ask why I got no answer to my invitation?

Lawrence (*off*) Frieda sent you a message.

Mabel (*off*) This! This dirty little piece of torn paper. "Not coming to supper, so sorry Frieda." Neither one of you had the common courtesy to walk up to the camp, the decency to——

Lawrence (*off*) Mabel, you are impertinent! How dare you walk in here and accuse me in this damnable impudent way. How dare you! Leave my house. Get out!

Brett and Frieda scramble hastily out of the house and back on to the porch

Lawrence, brandishing the skinned rabbit backs Mabel threateningly into the room

This isn't Mabeltown you know. You are a guest up here. I'm not one of your subjects! You always have to dominate. Always impose your will. I tell you, Mabel, your will is like a whip! Or like a snake coiled up inside you. It revolts me.

Mabel (*tremulously*) How can you say that?

Lawrence Oh that's so like you, Mabel. You burst in here dying for a fight, insult me, talk to me about decent behaviour, then the minute the fight starts it's, "oh how can you say that?"

Mabel (*starting to cry*) That's not fair!

Lawrence Fair? It's bunk, that's what it is, it's all bunk! You want to take me over, you want me to submit to that snake of your will. Well, I'm sick of it. *Basta* to all that. *Basta! Basta!*

Mabel (*sinking on to the divan; sobbing*) Oh Lorenzo . . .

Lawrence (*a bit daunted*) There's no need to cry like that, Mabel. Don't take on. (*He sits down rather uncomfortably on the end of the divan*)

Mabel I can't help it.

Lawrence (*stern but not unkind*) You've never known the difference between self control and self discipline. Self control is all wrong, bad and wrong. It's you making yourself into a little mechanical god and imposing the illusion of your will over your blood.

Mabel (*with luxuriant sobs*) Oh yes yes, that's true . . .

Lawrence You say yes in your *head*, Mabel, that's where you know things. Like the captain on the bridge—imprisoned up there without knowing it's a prison. The captain thinks he's got all the power, trotting up and down in that tiny place giving orders. He's running the whole show! He knows nothing of what's below him and around him, the great surges and thunders of the sea, all that mysterious world full of the real life, the terrible important real power. He's afraid of it so he denies its existence— just as you do, Mabel.

Mabel Oh don't, Lorenzo, don't don't . . .
Lawrence (*enjoying it*) I'm not saying these things because I enjoy saying
them, Mabel. They must be said. You must come to understand that your
will is wicked and destructive and dry. You must kill that snake, Mabel.
Can you do it?
Mabel Oh I'll try, Lorenzo, just don't be cruel to me.
Lawrence Only to be kind.
Mabel Yes . . . yes . . .

*Mabel allows herself one last spasm of sobs and then, Lawrence watching with
his arms folded, she sits up, dries her eyes and blows her nose*

(*In a weak voice*) Oh I feel wonderful.

Outside Frieda and Brett exchange a look

Lawrence Now then. You stay and have tea with us, Mabel.
Mabel (*humbly*) Thank you, Lorenzo.
Lawrence Hand me that rabbit.

Mabel hands Lawrence the rabbit gingerly

I'll go and put the kettle on. Tell Frieda we'll have it out there. And after
tea you can teach me that song.

Lawrence goes out to the kitchen

Mabel goes out on to the porch

Frieda (*solicitously*) Are you all right, Mabel? You look terrible.
Mabel Lorenzo was angry with me.
Frieda Oh was he? (*Shouting down Brett's ear trumpet*) Lorenzo was angry
with Mabel.
Brett (*sympathetically*) Oh.
Mabel (*saintly*) Yes but it's all right now.
Brett Sorry, Mabel, what did you say?
Mabel (*still gentle, slightly louder*) I said it's all right now.
Brett All what?
Mabel (*snapping*) All right!

Lawrence comes out on to the porch

Lawrence The tea's mashing. We're having the jam from those blackberries
you picked, Brett.
Frieda And me! I picked them too.
Lawrence All right, all right. (*He walks downstage gazing out*) Never never
will I get used to this astonishing view. It's always beautiful at any hour of
the day. The clouds . . . this huge sky. Look at the desert down there, miles
of it like some old magic kingdom and the great blue mountains beyond
it. I feel such a . . . damn!
Mabel What's wrong?
Lawrence It's Susan. She's got out of the field again, look. Blast that
infuriating cow! Come on, quick—we'll have to catch her. Frieda, you

come with me. Brett, Mabel, go round that way and stop her getting into the woods.

Brett Yes, Lorenzo. Hurry, Mabel!

Brett rushes off

Mabel I am!

Mabel follows Brett off

Lawrence I'll kill that creature one day, I swear I will. She only does it to madden me.

Lawrence and Frieda exit

(*Off*) Oh hang on, I'd best have the rope.

Lawrence enters, gets the rope and starts off

(*Extravagantly*) What have I done to deserve this persecution?

Black-out

During the Black-out the four Students and the Professor enter with their chairs and sit on them upstage

Other furniture is struck during the Black-out

One spot comes up on Lawrence. He stands frozen during the following, which is the recorded voice of Student IV

Student IV's voice . . . and was, as he saw it, consistently persecuted by the critics throughout his working life. Reviews for *The Rainbow* published in nineteen fifteen. "A monstrous wilderness of phallicism!" "A mass of obscenity of thought, idea and action!" "Windy, tedious and nauseating!" "An orgy of sexiness that omits no form of viciousness!" Then in nineteen twenty-one came the reviews for *Women in Love.* "This novel is sub-human and bestial!" "An epic of vice!" "An obscene abomination!" In nineteen twenty-eight *Lady Chatterley's Lover.* Once more the critics attacked. "The most evil outpouring that has ever besmirched the literature of our country!" "An abysm of filth!" "The sewers of French pornography would be dragged in vain to find a parallel in beastliness!" "Here is dirt in festering putrid heaps!" (*Pause*) From the first critical response in nineteen eleven to——

Student IV is violently interrupted by Lawrence who brings the rope up over his head and cracks it down on the stage

Immediately the Lights come up on stage

Lawrence Critics—*canaille! Canaglia! Schweinhunderei!* They stink in my nostrils. A curse, a murrain, a pox on this crawling, sniffling, spunkless brood of humanity! I am not very much moved. I'm beyond that now. I only curse them all, body and soul, root branch and leaf to eternal damnation!

Frieda enters, carrying a suitcase

Frieda I don't know why you let them upset you, Lorenzo. What do they matter?

Lawrence They are evil minded little beetles. They're smug, bigoted, illiterate——

Frieda has taken the rope from Lawrence and is tying it around the suitcase

Frieda So? All the more reason why they shouldn't prevent you from being in your own country.

Lawrence I don't want to be in my own country. Remember, I will not stay longer than a month, Frieda.

Frieda Ja ja, Lorenzo, you keep telling me that. Oh this stupid thing.

Lawrence We wouldn't be going to London at all if it weren't for those children of yours. Here, let me do it. That's no good. (*He kneels down and takes over the tying*)

Frieda OK. (*She gets up and starts off*) It'll only be a fortnight or so and then we'll go to my mother in Baden Baden.

Frieda goes

Lawrence (*shouting after her*) Oh you've decided everything, of course.

Frieda (*off*) Don't be silly, Lorenzo. You are the one who decided we should go. I'm only doing what you want.

Lawrence (*bad-temperedly to himself*) What I want! Bossy overbearing Prussian. (*He finishes tying up the case and stands. Looking out he sees something and calls*) Frieda.

Frieda enters. She's wearing a cape and a hat and is carrying a dowdy tweed jacket and a hat for Lawrence. She's also got Lawrence's stool

Frieda What?

Lawrence (*pointing up*) Look, an eagle.

They stand in silence looking upwards together

Frieda He's gone.

Lawrence Yes.

Frieda puts down the stool

Frieda We forgot your stool when we were tying up the furniture.

Lawrence (*shrugging*) Well, it'll get eaten by the packrats then.

Frieda Hal and Spud will keep it for us till we get back.

Lawrence Yes, all right. (*Looking around*) I hate to leave this place. I wish we didn't have to go.

Frieda helps Lawrence on with his coat and gives him his hat

Frieda We'll be back in the Spring. It's too cold here for your lungs in the winter, Lorenzo. You——

Lawrence (*edgily*) My bronchials. There's nothing the matter with my lungs.

Frieda Yes. Anyway we'll find somewhere warm for the winter. (*Gently she brushes down the front of his coat*) The first snow will be coming soon. (*She looks out*) Look how dark the sky is over the——

A loud blast on a whistle from off-stage is heard

Lawrence (*jumping*) My God!

Frieda (*angrily*) Brett!

Brett enters and blows another blast on the whistle

Lawrence All right, Brett, all right! We know you're here.

Brett gets out her ear trumpet and trots over to him

Brett Sorry, Lorenzo, what?

Lawrence Nothing nothing nothing.

Frieda (*loudly*) Nothing!

Brett Bill Hawk is on his way up with the wagon. Will you be stopping at Mabel's to say goodbye?

Lawrence No.

Brett (*smugly*) I thought not.

Frieda Oh it's all bosh. Childish! It's not just Mabel's fault, these stupid fights. Lawrence is not perfect, Brett, if you hadn't noticed. He's not a saint.

Brett But she's been saying terrible things. All about Lorenzo exploiting her and taking away her friends and betraying the Indians in his books——

Frieda And? And? What does he say about her? He says she is power mad and full of poison, he says she bullies and lies and is hysterical and she should be feathered and tarred and ridden out of Taos on a rail. He——

Lawrence I never said that.

Brett (*earnestly*) Well you did, Lorenzo. I remember it was when——

Lawrence (*shouting*) All I want is a last look at the ranch to say goodbye and all you women can do is clatter and gossip and——

Frieda Oh not goodbye. It isn't, Lorenzo. *Au revoir*, that's all. *Auf wiedersehen*. Isn't it, Brett?

Brett (*surprised*) Of course. You'll be back in the spring. Did you get all the furniture tied up to the rafters?

Frieda Only we forgot this. (*She points to stool*) But I'm going to ask——

Brett (*picking it up*) I'll keep it for you.

Frieda (*trying to get it back*) No thank you Brett, I——

Brett (*keeping it*) It's quite all right. No bother.

Frieda Brett! I said——

Lawrence (*exasperated*) You see? There you go again.

Frieda lets go of the stool

Frieda (*sulking*) Anyway as soon as we get back to Europe Lorenzo and Mabel will be writing those long letters to each other.

Lawrence I shall certainly not write letters to Mabel.

Brett (*stoutly*) She doesn't deserve it.

Frieda You will because you always do. Ach, so many letters. All about psychology and philosophy and Mabel's wonderful book and Mabel's fascinating soul . . .
Lawrence (*sharply*) Shut up, Frieda. You're being childish.
Frieda Oh ho ho, I am being childish, am I? I suppose I am the one who——

The sound of a horse and wagon off stage is heard

Oh, there's Bill. (*Anxiously*) Have we got everything, Lorenzo? It's time to go. I'd better take him this.

Frieda picks up the suitcase but Lawrence takes it from her

Lawrence I'll take it. It's too heavy for you. (*Affectionately*) Don't worry. Don't get in a state.
Frieda (*smiling gratefully at him*) I'll go and ask him to load up the trunks.

Frieda goes

Lawrence Now Brett, when you've finished typing those stories——
Brett I'll send them straight to Curtis Brown in London.
Lawrence No no no, to me. I shall need to proof them. I'll send an address as soon as I know where we'll be.
Brett Right. To you. Yes, Lorenzo.
Lawrence And mind you register the parcel, Brett. And for God's sake do try and keep your spelling something like mine.
Brett I'll try.
Lawrence And write and let me know when you need more money for feed for the horses.
Brett Yes I will. And I'll catch the chickens this afternoon and take them down to Bill's.
Frieda (*off stage*) Lorenzo! Bring the suitcase.
Brett I'll take it.
Lawrence No, Brett——

Brett grabs the suitcase and trots off

Lawrence shrugs and lets Brett go. He looks around and sighs

Lawrence All the dozens and dozens of places Frieda and I have lived— always paying rent. This is the only place we've ever owned. (*He walks downstage, looking out. Then almost inaudibly*) I wish we weren't going. (*He stands, silent*)

Brett enters again, watches him, then moves toward him

Brett (*troubled*) Lorenzo . . .
Frieda (*off, shouting*) Lorenzo!
Lawrence (*calling*) I'm coming. (*He starts off, just barely pausing when he sees Brett*) Goodbye, Brett. Take care of yourself.

Lawrence goes

Frieda (*off, calling*) Cheerio Brett. Bye-bye.

Lawrence (*off*) Goodbye.

Sound of the horse and wagon going off. Brett, holding the stool, waves

Brett Goodbye ... goodbye ...

Brett hugs the stool as she stands watching them go. Then she puts it down and sits on it. As she does this, Student II stands up and begins to read from her notebook. Brett freezes

Student II ... and not only were all his spiritual, moral and sexual teachings rejected and ridiculed but most of the critics of the day completely denied his literary merit. E. M. Forster disagreed. He said, quote: "he was the greatest imaginative novelist of our generation," close quote. To which T. S. Eliot replied, quote: "unless we know exactly what Mr Forster means by greatest, imaginative and novelist, I submit that the judgement is meaningless", close quote. In fact it wasn't until after the Second World War that Lawrence came into his own as writer and prophet. He became one of the most popular writers in the world and young people everywhere adopted him as a——

Brett suddenly looks up

Brett (*calling out*) That just isn't true. You've got it quite quite wrong.

Student II immediately sits down

Mabel enters carrying a box of papers and a cushion

Mabel Brett, I am only telling you what Lorenzo told me himself. These so-called friends of his gave a dinner party for him at the Café Royal. Lorenzo didn't even want to go but they insisted. They all got terribly drunk—Lorenzo wasn't drinking at all himself—and all of them swore they'd come to New Mexico with him. But, as he said to me, he saw right through them. He knew perfectly well that they'd all betray him and abandon him and he just put his head down on the table and wept and wept.

Brett He didn't weep, he was sick.

Mabel I'm sorry but I simply don't believe that. Anyway what do you know about it?

Brett I was there.

Mabel (*dashed*) Oh. You were? Well of course your point of view could easily have——

Brett (*raising her voice*) Which means that there is yet another glaring inaccuracy in your book.

Mabel (*with poisonous sweetness*) Well I don't think I'd talk about inaccuracies in books if I were *you*, Brett. And incidentally I can't tell you how ridiculous you look sitting on Lorenzo's stool. Quite frankly I don't understand why you ever got that stool. I mean Frieda must——

Brett Lorenzo gave it to me.

Mabel (*sarcastically*) Oh did he?

Brett Yes. The day they left the ranch.

Mabel (*with a complete change of mood*) Oh dear. (*She sits down on the cushion and holds the box on her lap. She speaks sadly*) We never even said goodbye that day. The last time.

Brett (*patting Mabel rather awkwardly*) Well. You and Lorenzo were always having those silly rows.

Mabel And it was so stupid! Because of course there we were writing each other long long letters within a month after they left. (*Picking up some papers in the box*) I can't find that one. I've looked all the way through. I swear there was one saying he wanted to be buried by that tree.

Brett Well, he was buried in France.

Mabel Yes I know, but if she's going to bring his ashes back here——

Brett She *has* brought them back. Or at least horrible fat little Angelino has.

Mabel And nearly didn't, Brett! Would you believe it—Frieda's daughter told me that first of all he almost let the New York customs take them off him and *then* when he got off the train at Santa Fe, he left the urn on the station platform!

Brett No! Oh poor Lorenzo . . . when you think. So humiliating to be treated like that by Frieda's . . . (*She hesitates*)

Mabel Lover! That's what he is, Brett. All that flapdoodle about "my *friend*, Angelino". And I happen to know she's started up with him before Lorenzo even died!

Brett Oh no, Mabel.

Mabel Oh yes! Barby told me. "Well," I said to her, "Your mother can't really help herself, she just is a very very physical woman." I *said*. "At her age you would think she'd be satisfied getting you and your brother and sister back into her life but no, she's insatiable." I told Barby about our plan.

Brett You didn't! You're mad!

Mabel Oh fuss fuss. She's on our *side*, Brett. She loathes Angelino. And she really did love Lorenzo. She was there when he died.

Brett Well I know that, but——

Mabel Can you imagine? She told me that Angelino was so rude to her the other night that she threw a glass at him and he slapped her!

Brett Oh! The little beast.

Mabel Now the thing is, Brett, do we know when Frieda's actually having this memorial service affair?

Brett Yes. Next Thursday. She——

Frieda enters in a furious rage

Frieda So! Here you are, plotting and planning. Oh, you evil women.

Mabel Frieda!

Frieda Aren't you ashamed? Grave robbers!

Brett What *are* you talking about?

Frieda Barby has told me everything.

Mabel Oh, that little snake in the grass!

Brett You see? What did I say?

Frieda I never thought you would go so far. When he was alive you were bad enough, both of you, grabbing and clutching at him—always thinking you could take him away from me. But to steal his ashes! It's grotesque!

Mabel Those ashes should be buried at the foot of the old pine tree.

Brett No they shouldn't. They should be scattered over the desert.

Mabel Brett! I thought we agreed that——

Brett Well we didn't. I *know* that's what he would have wanted.

Frieda The ashes are going into the shrine.

Mabel Shrine! A hideous little tourist attraction. Lorenzo would have detested it. I suppose you're going to charge admission, are you, Frieda?

Brett Ugh. Chapel of Rest. Anyway it looks like a public lavatory.

Frieda It does not! It's going to be beautiful when Angie's finished it.

Brett (*scathing*) Do you ever notice the contrast between your "Angie" and the man who was your husband? The great genius who would have been injured to the bottom of his soul to see his "grieving widow" cuddling and kissing with that greasy little dago?

Mabel (*sweetly*) Now Brett, Frieda can't help her nature you know. And of course when you're fifty-six there isn't that much choice around.

Frieda (*stung*) You're fifty-six too!

Mabel Fifty-five. And I'm living with my husband. Who I love.

Frieda My husband is dead! And you know perfectly well that I loved my Lorenzo and he loved me.

Brett He's not your Lorenzo anymore, Frieda. He belongs to the world now.

Frieda Oh ja ja! Along with those awful smarmy books you and Mabel wrote about him. The minute he was dead both of you scribbling away to tell everybody how important you were to him. Lies and gossip and wish fantasies.

Mabel You wrote a book too!

Frieda (*loftily*) Somebody had to tell the truth.

Brett That? Romantic fairy stories. Lorenzo would have roared with laughter.

Mabel And you're very lucky I decided not to sue you for slander.

Brett Me too.

Frieda Ach I'm going. I don't want to listen to you or talk to you anymore, either of you. I only came to tell you not to go anywhere near those ashes. (*She starts out*)

Mabel And how are you going to stop us, Frieda? Are you going to mount an armed guard over them?

Brett Quite. Perhaps you can keep us away until after this potty little memorial service of yours which I wouldn't dream of going to——

Frieda You're not invited. You are both not invited.

Mabel Good. The whole thing is just a travesty.

Brett We'll get those ashes eventually, Frieda, if we have to wait years.

Frieda Oh do you think so? Well shall I tell you what Angelino's going to do? He's going to mix Lorenzo's ashes with sand and cement and out of it he's making an altar stone as big as this. (*She stretches out her arms*) For the shrine. I'd like to see you move that! (*She smiles at them and waggles her fingers as she goes*) Toodle pip.

Frieda goes

Brett It's all your fault, Mabel. Talking too much as usual.

Brett goes

Mabel picks up the cushion and the box and stands silent for a moment

The Lights go down on the house area

Mabel Rats!

Mabel goes

Student III stands and starts to read from her notebook

Student III ... while examining the whole crucial question of Lawrence's own sexuality. Certainly there is some evidence indicating repressed homosexuality. In Lawrence's prologue to his novel *Women in Love*—and this prologue was suppressed during his lifetime—he describes the main character, Rupert Birkin, who is accepted by critics and scholars as a self-portrait, in the following way, quote: "It was for men that he felt the hot, flushing, roused attraction which a man is supposed to feel for the other sex. The male physique had a fascination for him and for the female physique he felt only a fondness," close quote.

Off stage there is the sound of Lawrence and the three women singing very softly "Swing Low, Sweet Chariot"

In this paper I am going to discuss and analyse those passages in Lawrence's writing which point us towards the understanding of the attraction that homosexuality had for him. The naked wrestling scene in *Women in Love*, the massage sequence in *Aaron's Rod*, the relationship between Paul and Edgar in *Sons and Lovers* and also that between Ursula and Winifred in *The Rainbow*. All these——

The singing is getting gradually louder during the above

The Lights come up slowly on Lawrence, Frieda, Mabel and Brett, sitting on the steps. Their singing becomes so loud that Student III is drowned out entirely and she sits down

Lawrence Swing low, sweet chariot,
Frieda Coming for to carry me home.
Mabel Swing low, sweet chariot,
Brett Coming for to carry me home.

I looked over Jordan and what did I see
Coming for to carry me home?
A band of angels coming after me
Coming for to carry me home.

Swing low, sweet chariot, *etc.*

If you get there before I do,
Coming for to carry me home,
Tell all my friends I'm coming too
Coming for to carry me home.

Frieda Oh Mabel, that is such a nice one. I love that. Aren't there any more verses?

Mabel Yes but I can't remember them. It's ages since I sang that song.

Behind this Lawrence has started singing the German song Frieda sang in Act I. Frieda joins in. Brett and Mabel listen

Brett (*when they finish*) Beautiful.

Mabel You've got a wonderful singing voice, Frieda.

Frieda Danke, Mabel.

Brett Now let's sing "Row Row Row Your Boat".

Lawrence Ah, Brett's favourite.

Mabel But you always lose your place, Brett.

Brett I won't. I won't.

Brett starts to sing and the others join in for the round but Brett does get it wrong after a couple of times round and it collapses. They all laugh

Frieda You should be the best, Brett, because you can't hear the rest of us.

Brett I'm sorry. I'm hopeless.

Lawrence (*mock sternly*) You are. Absolutely hopeless. You're a failure, Brett.

Brett (*meekly*) Yes, Lorenzo. Next time we sing it I'll get it right, I promise.

Frieda (*laughing*) Oh my God! Yes Lorenzo, yes Lorenzo. You shouldn't let him call you names. I'd like to hear him call me a failure.

Lawrence Shall I? Shall I?

Mabel (*promptly*) No don't. We're all nice and peaceful.

Lawrence gets up, stretches and comes down off the steps and downstage

Lawrence It's a funny little round, that one. (*He hums it*)

Frieda Yes. I like that image, you know. Little innocent dreamy boats rowing and rowing through their lives. I think it's the soul bobbing along so merrily toward death.

Mabel (*pleased*) That's nice.

Lawrence (*fondly*) Great sloppy sentimental Hun.

Brett Like your poem, Lorenzo. (*She recites feelingly*)
Oh build your ship of death, your little ark,
and furnish it with food, with little cakes, and wine
for the dark flight into oblivion.

Lawrence Ah ha, you see, Frieda. I thought of it first.

Frieda (*laughing*) Trust you, Brett.

Mabel It's a wonderful poem.

Lawrence I've written worse. (*Then, remembering*)
We are dying, we are dying, piecemeal our bodies are dying

and our strength leaves us,
and our soul cowers naked in the dark rain over the flood
cowering in the last branches of the tree of our life.

We are dying, we are dying, so all we can do
is now to be willing to die, and to build the ship
of death to carry the soul on the longest journey.

Oh build your ship of death. Oh build it!
for you will need it.
For the voyage of oblivion awaits you.

They are all silent and Student IV enters the silence reading from his notebook

Student IV ... of advanced tuberculosis on March second, nineteen
hundred and thirty.

*The Lights fade on the house. Frieda and Lawrence stand. She remains on the
porch but turns her back to the audience. Lawrence goes down the steps and
stands downstage*

He never came back to New Mexico partly because he knew the
authorities would probably refuse him a visa on health grounds. However, even when he was dying of it, even in those last few days, he never
admitted to having tuberculosis. His hyper-sensitivity, his morbid depres-
sions and sudden rages were always blamed on circumstances or on other
people, never his lungs. We can see that chronic illness reveals itself in the
tendency for his prose to become febrile, repetitious, even hysterical.
There are, too, the intense and potent descriptions of nature. He saw the
plants, the animals, the landscapes with the heightened clarity of a dying
man. The last——
Mabel Listen Brett!

A spot comes up on Mabel. Student IV sits. Mabel holds up a letter

It's from Lorenzo. (*Reading*) "If we can manage it and I can come back to
the ranch then we can all begin afresh. A new life with real tenderness.
You must help me about coming over when the time comes. I think we
might all be a great soothing and support to one another, I do really."
(*She holds the letter to her breast and closes her eyes*) He's coming back.
It's been five years and he's finally coming back.
Brett Oh Mabel, listen. It's from Frieda. (*Reading*) "He's very ill. I am
almost despairing. He suffers much. I feel that the few who are fond of
him should be with him to buck him up. Now. Could you come over? We
must get him better again." (*She puts the letter down*) I would have gone. I
would have gone.
Mabel Yes.   •

*Now Frieda moves to stand beside Lawrence. They look at each other as they
speak*

Frieda Before he went to the sanatorium we were in our little rented villa over the Mediterranean. In his room there were flowering plants and a goldfish in a bowl. A big ginger cat had adopted us. Lawrence sat up in bed in his blue jacket, so weak but always writing, and the cat curled up near him sleeping. I said everything is growing and healthy and flourishing in this room, the plants, the goldfish, the cat—why can't you flourish too?

Lawrence I want to. I want to. Oh Frieda, why did we quarrel so much?

Frieda (*sadly*) Violent creatures that we were, how could we help it?

Lawrence (*after a pause*) I hate this sanatorium. Next to my room there's a young girl who cries out in the night ... "*Maman, Maman, je souffre tant!*" I want to leave. I want us to be by ourselves in our own place. I don't want to stay here.

Brett Do you remember that day when we were all baking bread together and he coughed up blood? A splash of bright red blood on the stones.

Mabel And none of us said anything. We pretended it hadn't happened. So did he.

Frieda So we found a comfortable little house and on March the first we took him there in a taxi. My daughter Barby came over from England and Ida Rauh was there and Aldous and Maria Huxley. It was the only time he allowed me to take his shoes off for him. He lay down on the bed he was to die on, exhausted.

Lawrence Don't leave me. Don't go away.

Frieda So I slept on the couch where he could see me.

Mabel When you think of him digging the irrigation ditch that summer ...

Brett And how he always rode his horse so fast.

Frieda The next day was Sunday and I sat by his bed all day. He was reading the life of Christopher Columbus. After lunch Aldous and Maria and Barby came to see him but at tea time he began to get worse.

Lawrence I must have a temperature, I am delirious. Give me the thermometer.

Frieda This was the only time, seeing his tortured face, that I cried.

Lawrence (*quickly; commanding*) Don't cry.

Frieda So I ceased to cry anymore.

Lawrence Get the doctor. I ought to have some morphine now.

Frieda And my daughter and Aldous went to get the doctor.

Lawrence Hold me, hold me, I don't know where I am! I don't know where my hands are ... where am I?

Frieda Then the doctor came and gave him an injection of morphine.

Lawrence I'm better now ... I'm better.

Frieda The minutes went by. I held his left ankle, it felt so full of life. All my days I shall hold his ankle in my hand.

Brett Bright bright blue eyes.

Mabel And that red beard.

Frieda He was breathing more peacefully and then suddenly there were gaps in the breathing and the moment came when the thread of his life tore in his heaving chest and death had taken hold of him. Lawrence, my Lorenzo, who had loved me and I him ... he was dead.

Lawrence turns to face out, his eyes closed. Frieda moves away from him, weeping

My love ... Oh my love ... my love ... oh my love.

Over this Brett sings very softly—and well—"Row Row Row Your Boat". Then Mabel joins her singing it as Frieda speaks the following

Then we buried him very simply, like a bird. (*Pause. Then remembering with pain*) What kind of bird is this? We put lots and lots of mimosa on his coffin and all I said was "Goodbye Lorenzo".

Brett and Mabel move up to stand beside Frieda

Music

Brett Goodbye, Lorenzo.
Mabel Goodbye, Lorenzo.

The Professor stands and addresses the Students. He's reading from a notebook

Professor ... for the next study weekend at Kiowa Ranch. Among those topics are: the attraction of Lawrence for aristocratic women, Lawrence as quasi-Christ figure, the use of four letter words in *Lady Chatterley's Lover*, the multi-dimensional present in Lawrence's world picture, fashion and the Lawrence heroine, Lawrence's phallic vision, Lawrence as——

He is interrupted as Lawrence speaks the following, starting quietly but becoming more emotional and reaching a kind of calm exultance at the end

The Light becomes brighter on him as it dims on the Students and the women

Lawrence   Not I, not I, but the wind that blows through me!
A fine wind is blowing the new direction of time.
If only I let it bear me, carry me,
          if only it carry me.
If only I am sensitive, subtle, oh delicate,
          a winged gift.
If only, most lovely of all, I yield myself
          and am borrowed
By the fine wind that takes its course through
          the chaos of the world
Like a fine, an exquisite chisel, a wedge-blade inserted;
If only I am keen and hard like the sheer tip of a wedge
Driven by invisible blows,
The rock will split, we shall come at the wonder, we shall
          find the Hesperides.

CURTAIN

FURNITURE AND PROPERTY LIST

ACT I

On stage: Skeletal representation of wooden house, with steps and a corral fence
Chairs, including crude wooden chair with painted decorations
Sketch pad and sketching utensils

Off-stage: Branch of tree **(Mabel)**
Chicken **(Frieda)**
Firewood **(Brett)**
Book **(Student IV)**
Papers, extra chairs (*if required*) **(Students)**
Stool, notebook **(Lawrence)**
Head-dress, blanket **(Mabel)**
Notepaper **(Brett)**
Book **(Mabel)**

Personal: **Brett:** Ear trumpet (*throughout*)
Lawerence: ring

Page 19

Set: **Mabel**'s living-room, chairs etc.

Off-stage: Cushions, dressing-up clothes box. *In it:* costumes, including dog-collars, red beard, various dresses, ribbons, hats, capes, shawls, blankets, homberg, black doctor's bag, etc. **(Lawrence and Brett)**
Victrola and records **(Student I)**

ACT II

Strike: **Mabel**'s living-room, chairs etc.

Set: Divan
Sewing materials
Book, cigarettes
Coil of rope

Off-stage: Gun, rabbit, bag containing painting **(Brett)**
Skinned rabbit **(Lawrence)**

Page 36

Strike: Furniture

Set: **Students'** chairs

Off-stage: Rope **(Lawrence)**
          Suitcase **(Frieda)**
          Jacket, hat, stool **(Frieda)**
          Whistle **(Brett)**
          Box containing papers, cushion **(Mabel)**

Personal: **Mabel:** handkerchief, letter
          Student II: notebook

LIGHTING PLOT

Act I

To open: Black-out

Cue 1	During opening dialogue, when ready *Gradually bring up lights, warm exterior*	(Page 1)
Cue 2	**Professor** and the **Students** exit *Fade to Black-out*	(Page 4)
Cue 3	**Lawrence:** "Brett!" *Bring up Lights on* **Lawrence**, *then whole stage, exterior day*	(Page 4)
Cue 4	**Brett** exits *Fade to Black-out*	(Page 6)
Cue 5	**Student IV:** ". . . pure white snow on the ground. . . ." *Bring up Lights on* **Students**	(Page 6)
Cue 6	**Student IV:** ". . . took off her blue robe." *Bring up Lights on* **Lawrence** *and* **Brett**	(Page 6)
Cue 7	**Frieda:** "What kind of a bird is this?" *Black-out except for Light on* **Student I**	(Page 12)
Cue 8	**Student I:** ". . . go and work in Germany. Thank you." *Snap up square of light on* **Lawrence** *and* **Frieda**	(Page 12)
Cue 9	**Student I:** "Next." *Black-out; after sound of slide, snap up square of light*	(Page 12)
Cue 10	**Student I:** "Next." *Black-out; after sound of slide, snap up square of light*	(Page 13)
Cue 11	**Student I:** "Next." *Black-out; after sound of slide, snap up square of light*	(Page 13)
Cue 12	**Student I:** "Next." *Black-out; after sound of slide, snap up square of light*	(Page 14)
Cue 13	**Student I:** "Next." *Black-out; after sound of slide, snap up square of light*	(Page 15)
Cue 14	**Student I:** "Next." *Black-out; after sound of slide, snap up square of light*	(Page 15)
Cue 15	**Student I:** "Oh, I'm sorry. Wrong slide." *Black-out; after sound of slide, snap up square of light. After a moment, Black-out*	(Page 15)
Cue 16	**Student I:** "No. That's right. That's right." *Snap up square of light*	(Page 15)

Cue 17	**Student I:** "Next."	(Page 15)
	Black-out; after sound of slide, snap up square of light	
Cue 18	**Lawrence** falls forward	(Page 16)
	Black-out	
Cue 19	**Student I:** "Lights, please."	(Page 16)
	Full lights up	
Cue 20	**Mabel** exits	(Page 18)
	Lights change	
Cue 21	**Student IV:** "No!"	(Page 28)
	Black-out except for pool of light centring on **Student IV**	
Cue 22	**Frieda** puts her arms around **Student IV**	(Page 28)
	Fade pool of light	
Cue 23	**Frieda:** "Oh my love, my love ... oh my love."	(Page 28)
	Black-out	

Act II

To open: Black-out

Cue 24	When ready	(Page 29)
	Bring up general lighting, exterior, warm	
Cue 25	**Lawrence:** "What have I done to deserve this persecution?"	(Page 36)
	Black-out; when ready, bring up spot on **Lawrence**	
Cue 26	**Lawrence** cracks the rope	(Page 36)
	Snap up general lighting	
Cue 27	**Brett** exits. **Mabel** picks up cushion, stands silent	(Page 43)
	Fade lights on house area	
Cue 28	**Student III:** "The naked wrestling scene in *Women in Love* ..."	(Page 43)
	Gradually bring up Lights on house area	
Cue 29	**Student IV:** "March second, nineteen hundred and thirty."	(Page 45)
	Fade Lights on house area	
Cue 30	**Mabel:** "Listen, Brett!"	(Page 45)
	Light on **Mabel**	
Cue 31	**Lawrence:** "Not I, not I ..."	(Page 47)
	Bring up pool of light on Lawrence, fade general light gradually	
Cue 32	**Lawrence:** "... we shall find the Hesperides."	(Page 47)
	After a moment, Black-out	

EFFECTS PLOT

ACT I

Cue 1   **Student II:** "Yes, but my overall interest ..."   (Page 9)
Gradually fade up horse galloping in the distance, then getting nearer

Cue 2   **Professor:** "No, I don't think so."   (Page 10)
Horse galloping is very loud. Snap off sound

Cue 3   **Student I:** "Next." Black-out   (Page 12)
Noise of slide changing

Cue 4   **Student I:** "Next." Black-out   (Page 13)
Noise of slide changing

Cue 5   **Student I:** "Next." Black-out   (Page 13)
Noise of slide changing

Cue 6   **Student I: "Next."** Black-out   (Page 14)
Noise of slide changing

Cue 7   **Student I:** "Next." Black-out   (Page 15)
Noise of slide changing

Cue 8   **Student I:** "Next." Black-out   (Page 15)
Noise of slide changing

Cue 9   **Student I:** "Oh, I'm sorry. Wrong slide." Black-out   (Page 15)
Noise of slide changing

Cue 10   **Student I:** "Next." Black-out   (Page 15)
Noise of slide changing

Cue 11   **Lawrence** falls forward. Black-out   (Page 16)
Bring up café music, babble of voices and sound of vomiting

Cue 12   **Frieda** puts a record on   (Page 22)
Music

Cue 13   **Frieda** goes to gramophone and lifts the needle   (Page 23)
Cut music

ACT II

Cue 14   **Student III:** "... fundamental fear of women——"   (Page 29)
Distant gunshot

Cue 15*   **Frieda:** "... Look how dark the sky is over the——"   (Page 38)
Loud blast of whistle

Cue 16   **Frieda:** "... I suppose I am the one who——"   (Page 39)
Horse and wagon approaching

Cue 17 **Lawrence** (*off*): "Goodbye." (Page 40)
    Horse and wagon leaving

Cue 18* **Student III:** ". . . only a fondness, close quote." (Page 43)
    Singing

* *These effects may be produced by the actors at the director's discretion.*

MADE AND PRINTED IN GREAT BRITAIN BY
LATIMER TREND & COMPANY LTD PLYMOUTH
MADE IN ENGLAND